An Engineer's Guide to Silicon Valley Startups
3rd Edition

Piaw Na

This edition of the book is dedicated to my son, Bowen Na

Contact Information:
Piaw Na, 1453 Hampton Drive, Sunnyvale, CA 94087
E-mail: piaw.na@gmail.com
Web: http://books.piaw.net

I am committed to fixing any errors in this book. If you find any, please e-mail me at the above address. You will receive a copy of the next edition of the book.

Contents

0

Overview

Who am I?

I'm a software engineer who's worked at Silicon Valley startups for my entire career. They included:

- Geoworks, a maker of operating systems for IBM-compatible PCs. Geoworks IPOed in 1994.

- Pure Software, a maker of software development tools. Pure Software IPOed in 1995.

- Mpath Interactive/HearMe, an online service specializing in fast-twitch games. Mpath IPOed in 1999.

- Escalate, an e-commerce service provider. Escalate was sold for pennies on the dollar to a customer.

- Mirapoint, a maker of e-mail appliances for businesses and internet service providers. Mirapoint was shuttered.

- Google, a search engine company. Google IPOed in 2004.

In each case, I joined as a pre-IPO employee and, as a result, learned about how Silicon Valley startups work. The last chapter covers my personal experiences in detail.

Entrepreneurship

Joining a startup isn't the same as founding one. There're plenty of articles on the web that cover founder's issues such as interpreting term sheets and negotiating with venture capitalists. This book tells you what you need to know about joining and working at a startup, even if you're the very first employee.

Who is this book for?

This book is for engineers interested in joining an early stage startup, or considering a startup's offer. Since it takes engineers to build the actual product, they tend to be the bulk of a startup's early hiring.

When Google acquired Dodgeball, it dumped the founders into the product management organization but didn't give them engineers. It didn't take very long before the founders left the organization. Without any assigned engineers, they found it impossible to get anything built! Thus, the sections on interviewing at and evaluating startups mostly apply to engineers.

However, non-engineers will find this book's other advice useful, such as about stock options. In particular, if your startup is preparing to go public, you should read the sections on Tax Planning starting on page 83 as soon as possible.

How to use this book

I organized this book by one's chronological experience with a startup, starting with what you should know when considering if you should join any startup. Then how to get a job at a startup, etc., ending with leaving a startup. If you're already at a startup, you could skip over the first few chapters and first read about what to do while at a startup and how to do tax planning (but you should go back and read those first chapters before you go to your next startup!). Note that the eve of your big IPO is too late to read about tax planning.

In each chapter's bibliography, I provide shortened URLs (starting with http://goog.ly) for readers of the paperback to access the cited resources. If you'd prefer not to type them, http://books.piaw.net/guide/bibliography.html has a comprehensive set of clickable links.

1

Are Startups For You?

If you read many startup books or websites, you'll wonder why everyone isn't working for a startup. They're more exciting, you have more control over your destiny, and it seems more fun than a nine to five grind. This chapter tells you why a startup might or might not be right for you, and who does best in startups.

What is a startup?

When people talk about startups, they usually mean a pre-IPO company. The reality is that many pre-IPO companies aren't really startups. My favorite example is Perforce, which supports, sells, and licenses the same named source control program. While it's privately held, it has a mature business model, a solid revenue stream, and, more importantly, is unlikely to grow dramatically or go public except by selling itself to a bigger, already public, firm. In fact, while Perforce is a very successful business and extremely profitable for its owners, it's the antithesis of what most people mean when they say **startup.**

A startup (in the typical Silicon Valley sense):

- Is a relatively new venture (under 10 years old).

- Is funded by angel investors or venture capitalists (VCs), rather than fully owned by its founders.

- Expects to enjoy rapid growth after initial product design and implementation of its business.

- Expects to either make a big impact or, as many folks like to say, "Make a big crater in the ground from the crash."

- Has a new, rapidly-growing, market or completely disrupts an existing market.

Many people think startups either have a liquidity event or fail within five years, but that applies only to software startups. Hardware startups take longer. On the other hand, Google took six years to IPO, and could have delayed its IPO indefinitely.

Many Silicon Valley insiders tend to add one last controversial feature to the above list:

- The company isn't profitable yet.

I tend to discount this one as I've seen companies move in and out of profitability. I've also seen companies become profitable quickly, but not get enough business to be a long term success.

Why angels or VC money?

Entrepreneurs often wonder what kinds of businesses venture capitalists will fund. The best answer I've heard came from renowned VC Don Valentine, as paraphrased by Brian Apgar:

> "If you and your brother decide to go start a laundromat, that's a business somewhere around $100,000 to $500,000 a year in revenue. It could be very profitable, especially for you and your brother, but that's not the kind of business that a VC would fund. If you and a group of like-minded professionals got together and formed a consulting company, that's a $20 million to $40 million business, but it's not a fundamentally scalable business—every time you add customers you'll have to add more people. That's not the kind of business a VC would want either. A venture capitalist wants to fund corporations—companies that have the potential to have revenues of $100 million or more, and that build products that can be sold

repeatedly without having to add more scarce resources—in other words, a scalable business model."

VCs look for scalability because startups are inherently risky. Even that laundromat is risky—most small businesses don't survive their first year. Because they expect only a 10% company success rate, those 10% have to be so successful as to more than make up for the 90% that are failures! After all, the VCs are in this to make a profit.

This is the main reason businesses traditionally organized as partnerships, such as consulting and law firms, rarely get venture funding. Successful ones require the scarce resource of very talented people, and such firms

Why Silicon Valley?

While much of this book applies to startups anywhere, I chose to emphasize Silicon Valley. There are many reasons for this, the main one being that my entire career has been in Silicon Valley, and I couldn't possibly write authoritatively about the startup environments in Boston, New York, Seattle, or elsewhere. If you have startup experiences outside Silicon Valley, please share them by joining the mailing list at http://groups.google.com/group/startup-guide

Silicon Valley is unique in how it welcomes startups. For example, when Reed Hastings began working on Purify, he was consulting for Adaptive Corporation. Not only was Adaptive supportive, its CEO gave Pure Software creditability by endorsing Purify to her social network.

When Pure needed to expand its office space, it turned out their landlord was a big fan of UNIX software companies (yes, the landlord), and thought they were the future. He offered them a reduced rent in exchange for stock in the company.

Frequently, Silicon Valley attorneys, accountants, and other necessary facilitators will take a mixture of stock and cash as compensation from startups instead of charging full price. Silicon Valley's startup ecosystem is unparalleled with respect to how frequently startups are worked with and understood.

When I decided it was time to leave Escalate, Inc, it didn't take me long to find another startup. The risk of joining a Silicon Valley startup is very low; if it fails, there's another one around the corner.

If you decide that startups aren't for you any more, large Silicon Valley companies are happy to take you on board. In fact, those large companies prize entrepreneurial people such that startup experience frequently gives you an edge with them.

usually can't easily scale to a large size.

Good fits for startups

People who enjoy working at startups usually have at least a few of these attributes:

- **Impatience**. Such people get frustrated by big company bureaucracy, and dislike either waiting their turn or being bottlenecked on some resource or somebody else's work. Note that just because you can't concentrate on one project for long or get bored easily doesn't mean a startup is for you. Most startups have a long development period on their initial product before its launch. During that period you'll not working on anything else.

- **Jack of all trades**. At a startup, if you're frustrated by somebody else's work, but still want to make headway in your goals, you've usually got to be willing to do another person's work if necessary. If you're an engineer, you might have to make sales calls, take support questions, or even serve as the IT department. But as a business gets larger and more employees are hired, there's too much pressure to specialize and let specialists do their jobs since that's more efficient—even if one or two projects have to wait their turn before getting service. At larger companies, jacks and jills of all trades may not get to exercise their flexibility or multiple skills.

- **Adaptability**. Change is the mantra of most startups, and if you don't deal well with it, you probably won't be happy. Most startups will change business plans and radically recast products before achieving success. Mike Samuel joined a robotics startup—only to discover when he started that their most successful product was an expert system. Later, Google bought the entire company in order to use the system as a framework for internal applications. Google tried many paths to profitability, including selling the Google Search Appliance machine to enterprises, before Adwords took off.

Good reasons to join a startup

- You already know the people at the startup and think you'll enjoy working with them. Life's too short to work with people you don't like. If the startup fails, you don't want to regret those years spending hours and hours with folks you don't enjoy being with. I've worked at startups where the people involved were so comfortable with each other that we would work a full week, go sailing for a 3 day weekend, and come back and work the rest of the week—and still enjoy each other's company after that. Compared to large companies, startup product development teams are extremely stable. So if you like the team, you'll get to enjoy it for a long time.

- You've got an idea you want to work on, and the startup will allow you to do so. This is surprisingly common, since many startups still have the flexibility to accommodate better ideas at an early stage. Of course, if it's a bad idea, as soon as that's obvious expect it to be dropped like a hot potato.

- You believe in the technology or product they've built. This is surprisingly difficult to judge. For instance, before becoming part of AJAX, Javascript was a terribly implemented toy language. It took several iterations of browsers and better interpreters, as well as faster processors, before it could be used as it is today. Netscape, which introduced Javascript, went nowhere. On the other hand, one could see that the technology behind Google's search engine (large, cheaply built, clusters of computers dynamically allocated to jobs) could apply easily to many other problem spaces.

- They've got a great product you're excited about. Google is one obvious example. Nearly everyone who used Google after years with other search engines felt like a genius for being able to answer almost any question so quickly. The first time I used Purify, I realized we had a great product. Great products are ultimately what drive a startup to success and the big leagues. If you're not excited about the company's products, you probably have no business working there.

Bad reasons to join a startup

- To become fabulously wealthy. Ironically, the most lucrative startup I joined was also the largest. When I started at Google. it had 1500 people and wasn't much of a startup. But because most of the risk was already out of the business and the company was still private, my returns were still very good. A typical startup takes 3-4 years to prove itself. So unless the work itself is interesting and you enjoy working with the people there, it's very hard to stay interested for that long if you're only in it for the possibility of wealth. In my experience, the best startups have the most interesting people and solve the most challenging problems for the largest number of people.

- They've got a good business idea. Business plans can change many times before a startup reaches profitability. For example, one could be executed first by another company. Competition among entrepreneurs and VCs to have first mover advantage in a new market often results in multiple companies being funded to address the same problem. For instance, both Mpath interactive and Total Entertainment Network were founded at almost the same time to address the online gaming market. Neither company was successful.

- To further your big company career. I've met a number of executives for whom a startup is a short cut to a VP slot or similar brass ring. The problem's that a startup is frequently a bad place for those who've gotten comfortable working at a larger organization. The problems of growing a startup are not the same as those of a large business trying to control expenses in a mature market. Such misfits frequently create problems both for the startup and themselves. I was at a startup when a marketing executive spent so much money on consultants that the company had to layoff engineers. The big company mentality didn't work well in this case.

- To have something to brag about at parties. I've lost count of the number of times I've had to tell people I've met that I'm working at a company they've never heard of. Ironically, the one time I did work for a well known company, I didn't want to brag about it, since everyone would assume I was fabulously wealthy. I ended up telling people I worked for a technology company, only admitting to working at Google if pressed.

Big companies are sometimes better

Soon after Pure Software's IPO, a friend of mine left for Microsoft. At that time, Microsoft had around 30,000 employees. After two years at Microsoft, he was still very happy. Pure had only a few projects he could work on. But at Microsoft, when he got bored with one project, he would switch projects and work on something fresh and exciting to him. Furthermore, Microsoft constantly hired a large influx of rookie engineers that he could mentor and lead, while Pure tended to hire experienced engineers.

Some companies are small because they've yet to grow. Others are small because the owners/founders are awful. If you have a bad manager in a small company, it may be harder or impossible to escape than at a big one. At a large company, you can transfer to another department to switch managers. At a startup, you'll most likely have to leave the company instead.

If you're an experienced engineer, a large company hiring you as an architect or other senior position could mean that you get to do a project's fun parts (the design and important coding) while you get to parcel out grunt work to more junior engineers who still find it interesting or challenging.

On the other hand, ten years later when Microsoft was at 60,000 employees, another friend turned down a Google engineering position to work there as an architect. He deeply regretted that decision, as Microsoft was both past its fast growth phase and had gotten so large that even a very senior level person had problems making changes.

Ultimately, your fit at a startup depends on whether you're comfortable without the structure, resources, and large teams that big companies can provide. Think of a big company as sailing on a large ship, where everyone has a specialty and a designated station, and don't usually venture outside their assigned roles. A startup is sailing on a small boat, where everyone has to pitch in and pull on ropes or steer, even if they've never done it before, because they were in the right place to do the job.

The green card conundrum

Many green card holders are reluctant to join a startup; they're reluctant to switch jobs, period. They think switching will reset their priority date. However, the immigration process is more flexible than most people think, making startups less risky for green card applicants than they might expect.

Immigration categories

Most software engineers fall into one of three categories for immigration into the US:

- EB-3, for bachelor's degree holders with less than 5 years of experience

- EB-2, for masters or PhDs holders, or bachelor's degree holders with more than 5 years of progressive experience. The progression should be demonstrated by letters of reference from employers prior to the company the candidate joined, preferably demonstrated by promotions. There cannot be breaks or gaps (for instance, a leave of absence of sabbatical). (See http://goo.gl/Nl2b4)

- EB-1, for workers of "extraordinary ability."

If you were born in a country (note that it's the country of birth that matters here, not the country of citizenship) without significant immigration into the US (say, Western Europe or Singapore), there is a big difference between EB-2 and EB-3, but not much between EB-2 and EB-1; both EB-2 and EB-1 usually grant a green card in short order. However, if you are from an impacted country such as China or India, then the differences between EB-3, EB-2, or EB-1 could be significant! Note that for all countries EB-3 is extremely backlogged and will result in a very long wait. You can look up the current status of immigration visas on visa bulletins at: http://goo.gl/uCvlx.

If you qualify for a National Interest Waiver (NIW), you can self-petition for a green card even without a job offer. Obviously, if that is the case you can join whatever startup you wish, as long as it retains your NIW status. Even if you do not have your PhD yet, you can apply for NIW status. The best way to do this is to have published recognized papers and have very strong letters of recommendation from existing faculty members at top universities.

One way for bachelor degree holders to qualify for EB2 status is to work for 5 years as an engineer, and then switch jobs or get a promotion to a different job within the same company. In addition to the 5 years of progressive experience, the requirement is that there should be a 51% difference in job responsibilities. Establishing this change can be done by splitting up the time spent on various activities for the former position and the new position. The difference in the change of percentage should be 51%. An easy way to demonstrate this is if you switched from an individual contributor role to being a manager, since managing people involves a significant amount of supervision. Similarly, as you climb the individual contributor ladder, the higher positions should demand significantly more time spent in design, architecture, and requirements analysis compared to that of lower positions. This switch to a faster track could easily get you a green card faster.

EB-1A: Since Kazarian vs USCIS, it has become very hard to get into the EB1-A or Oustanding Ability category. In many cases, extensive documentation on the candidate's abilities had to be established. As an example, a colleague of Santhosh Srinivasan needed to get three letters of reference from known authorities in the field (professors or researchers). Out of the three, at least one had to be from someone who had not worked with him and only knew about him through his work! Secondly, at least 50% of the work had to involve research. Thirdly, he had to be on program committees of well known conferences. Finally, he needed to have published extensively and the citation count for those publications had to be high.

If you hold a management position, you can apply for a L-1 visa and then qualify for the EB-1C or multinational executive/manager category. This category requires you to hold a management position in a company outside the US that belongs to the employer or is an affiliate or a subsidiary. It must be 3 years prior to the application and you must be employed for at least a year in that position. Usually, such employees move to the US on a L-1A or L-1B visa. There is usually no waiting period for the EB-1C application. You do not need to have a higher degree or MBA to qualify for this.

The Diversity Visa program is also a good way to get a green card. Every year, up to 55,000 diversity visas are granted through a lottery to individuals from countries which do not have large numbers of immigrants. To qualify you must:

- Be born in a country that is allowed to apply (see http://goo.

gl/3JiU)

- You must have a high school education (or equivalent) or two years of work experience over the past five years in an occupation that requires two years of training.

The practical training period

A foreign student graduating with a degree in Science, Technology, Engineering and Math (STEM degrees) in the US has a year after graduation during which he is considered to be doing "practical training" (OPT stands for Optional Practical Training). During this period, you're allowed to work in a field related to your training without the need for a H-1B visa. The OPT program has several restrictions:

- The training has to be directly related to the field study (i.e., no working for McDonald's if you have a computer science degree)

- The OPT period is for 12 months

- During the OPT period, you cannot be unemployed for more than 90 days, including weekends, unless you worked for 20 hours a week or more, at which point weekends do not count.

For STEM degree holders, you may extend the OPT period for another 17 months, subject to the following restrictions:

Your degree needs to be in the following list: http://goo.gl/g1N2C

- The employer must be on E-verify

- An additional 30 days of employment is allowed with the extension. Over the 29 month total period (12 months + 17 months extension), you can accrue 120 days of unemployment, including weekends.

However, the H-1B visas come with an annual quota attached, so you should push your future employers to start the application process as soon as possible in case you miss the current year's quota. The fiscal year starts from October 1st and ends September 30th. Each year, applications are accepted starting from the first working day in April. There are approximately 65,000 H1-Bs available (including 6,800 openings for people from Chile and Singapore that will go back to the main pool if unused) in the main pool, and 20,000 H1-Bs for advanced degree holders.

There are two different mechanisms for switching from OPT status to H1B:

- Change of Status. At the start of the fiscal year where the application has been approved, the status is automatically changed from F-1 to H1B. If the application was approved later in the fiscal year, then the change happens when it is approved.

- Consular Processing. A deadline is set for switching over from F-1 to H1B. The applicant has to visit the US consulate in his or her home country to receive approval. This is the less preferred option since you risk the visa officer at the consulate delaying or denying the visa, though it has the advantage that you can continue to be on the F-1 for longer and avoid paying social security and medicare, saving about 6% of your salary.

If you miss the current year window, either retain your own lawyer or stay on top of your employer's immigration law department so as not to miss the next year's opening date, which could change from year to year. There could be cases where you apply for a H-1B towards the end of your OPT. To cover the gap between the completion of your OPT and the start of the H-1B, the CAP-GAP regulations may allow you to have more than the allocated OPT period (see http://goo.gl/E2cQW).

The H-1B visa is valid for 3 years. After 3 years you can renew it with automatic approval. You must have applied for a green card before the start of the 6th year. Beyond the 6th year of the H-1B and L-1 visa, the visa can be extended only if an immigration application is under process. If the application is in the first or second stages and still pending, then the visa is extended by one year. As a result, the status has to be renewed annually. If the I-140 has been approved, then the visa will be extended 3 years at a time. Note that if you spent time outside the US (for personal or business reasons), then your visa will be extended by the amount of time you spent outside the U.S. At the 6 year mark, you need to show that you have applied for a green card before the start of the final year of the **and** renew the H-1B every year starting from your 6th year in order to stay in status.

You get one OPT per degree level: BS, MS, and PhD. Each new degree level grants you a new OPT period. Note that if you have a PhD and then go back for a masters you will not get a new OPT period!

Retaining your own immigration lawyer

One reason to retain your own immigration lawyer instead of using the employer-sponsored lawyer is that your own immigration lawyer could be more willing to file for a higher category rather than using the lower category. For instance, you can apply for EB-1 and EB-2 NIW simultaneously without harm to your chances of getting a green card, but many employers will not spend the extra money to do so.

In fact, there is an inherent conflict of interest between corporate-sponsored immigration departments and you: the sooner you get your green card, the sooner you can switch employers (especially to a startup), and the more likely it is that your employer would have to pay you more to keep you at your job. One of my friends did not get a green card even after 5 years at a large corporation, despite being from a non-impacted country, because despite frequent and repeated promotions to a high level, the immigration lawyers his employer retained did not refile his application as an EB-1 or EB-2.

You need to watch the Visa bulletin like a hawk, especially if you are an EB-2/EB-3 petitioner from India or China. The priority date occasionally resets to current for 1 month or so and then resets back to a date a few years earlier. If you catch the window, you may save a few years of waiting. For example, during July 2007, the EB-2 category I-485 status was set as current (in other words, all applications have been processed as approved or denied). One month later, the current date was set back to 2005 and then moved forward very slowly and till late 2011, the date was set as July 2007.

When can you switch jobs during the process

All immigration processes start with filing for the labor certificate, then filing I-140. While waiting for the I-140 to be approved, you cannot change jobs without resetting your priority date. Once the I-140 has been approved, you can switch jobs and retain your priority date according to

204.5(e). However, most people do not switch jobs while waiting for their priority date to advance until they can file form I-485 (adjustment of status). They would have to re-file their form I-140, and during the job-switch window, their opportunity to file form I-485 could arrive. Missing that window because the new I-140 has not been approved could cause them to have to wait for another window to open. If you do switch jobs during this period, the onus is on you to stay on top of your new I-140 filing so that the application does not get lost and you lose your priority date and get reset.

Once your I-485 has been approved, you effectively have a green card. However, you're not out of the woods yet! There's a 180 day waiting period during which you should not switch jobs.

Most people hold valid H-1 status while filing I-485, so in theory they can switch job by transferring the H-1. However, two things could happen:

- You file "change of job" and that might trigger a RFE(request for evidence). Cindy Zhou noted that she had that twice for no apparent reason after she filed her I-485. RFEs may delay your I-485 approval process. This frequently results in a delay in issuing your Employment Authorization Document (EAD) and Advanced Parole (AP).

- You have to go out of country. The H-1 is non-immigrant status. You can apply for a visa and they don't question your "intent to return to home country". Once you filed for I-485, your intent to immigrate is clear. Hence you are required to have the AP to ensure that you can come back to US. Once you've declared the intent to immigrate, then applying for a H-1 visa to enter US puts you in a grey area. There are no case laws or regulations to follow in this grey area, and while many might have gotten away with this, I would consider it risky..

After you have gotten your EAD and AP and 180 days have passed (or you've received your green card), you can switch jobs without any concern. Before then, but after filing I-485, try to stay within the US.

Other risks

One of my friends changed from the California branch of a large corporation to the New York City branch of the same corporation. Because of
her location change, she was considered to have switched jobs and had
her priority date reset. In fact according to the law, if the company doesn't
revoke the application, and the application for I-140 has been approved
before switching jobs in the same company or between companies, she
can retain the priority date. One reason to retain your own immigration
lawyer would be to alert you to situations like this so you do not accept
such relocations without adequate compensation, as well as keeping your
employer honest!

Getting a green card through marriage

If you marry a US citizen or green card holder, you can get a green card
within 3-4 months. The process is straightforward if not simple: fill out

---

Starting your own company

When most people talk about startups, they really mean "I'm going to start
my own company." But the majority of people at startups are not founders.
While employees might not get the outsized rewards that founders get, they
also avoid things like having to rely on COBRA for health insurance. That's
one reason why many startups are founded by childless young people or
already independently wealthy folks. Starting your own company is outside
the scope of this book, but if you are doing so, this book might be useful in
helping you understand what your employees expect. They won't have the
same stake in your startup that you do.

---

forms I-140 and I-485 simultaneously, while having your spouse file form
I-130. (You will both have to supply form G-325a) There is no need to
retain an immigration lawyer as the instructions on the IRS website are
clear and the forms easy to understand. My wife and I did this in 2011
with minimal difficulty and no lawyer fees.

Finding the right startup

The single best way to join a startup is through a referral. Startups already carry lots of risk. They try to mitigate this by hiring carefully. If possible, they only hire people with a successful track record.

The best way to be someone folks at a new startup call is to cultivate and maintain the relationships you have with everyone you've met. Many people associate this with the dirty business of schmoozing and being a sleazeball, constantly selling yourself to everyone, and going to every party you can.

The reality is that if you're a good engineer, what it really means is maintaining your contact list and replying to e-mails from friends. Then, when you're out looking, you can send e-mail or use a social networking site like Facebook or LinkedIn to announce your availability. More likely, if people keep you in mind, they'll approach you with interesting new ventures that need people with your skills.

Most engineers are very bad at contact management. I once called a friend to recruit him for then pre-IPO Google. His response was "Darn. I should have called you earlier. I just accepted an offer from Amazon, sold my house, and am moving to Seattle next week."

Note that many companies have non-solicit agreements. That means if your friend at work just left for a startup, he's not going to call you about a fantastic open position at his new company. You have to take the initiative to contact him, have lunch, and learn about his new job. Even when meeting with you, he can't say "I've got the perfect position for you." But if you ask, "Does your startup have any openings for someone like me?", he can talk to you about them.

The next best thing is to work with a good recruiter, a.k.a. a headhunter. However, there's a huge difference between a good recruiter and a resume-spamming shop, and it's important to only work with recruiters with a good reputation:

- A recruiter should never send your resume to someone without your knowledge. Before doing so, they should always ask if you're interested in an opportunity.

- A recruiter should always be willing to tell you more about the company and what they do. If they can't answer your question, they can either find out, or arrange for you to meet with someone who can.

- A good recruiter shouldn't pressure you to take the job. That's always your decision. I look unfavorably upon high pressure tactics. Note that it's difficult for many recruiters to keep from doing this, since the company pays them a percentage of your salary if you get hired. If you don't take the job, they aren't paid.

My tack with recruiters is that I'm usually willing to discuss jobs with them, but only if they tell me what companies they're recruiting for. This lets me do independent research (for instance, looking at the company's website and seeing who they're funded by, what other jobs their managers have had, talking to people I know who work there, etc.) and not just get opinions from a biased source.

The last possibility is to cold call the company or submit your resume through its website. This is usually the lowest probability option, since many companies (especially well-known ones) receive upwards of 1000 resumes a day! The web has plenty of tips for this approach, so I won't go into more detail here.

The perception of risk

The elephant in the startup room is the risk involved. This gets magnified by entrepreneurs who enjoy justifying their out-sized rewards by the amount of risk they took. Folks then conflate that risk with the risk of being a startup employee. In practice, the risk isn't as high as the general public thinks, or that entrepreneurs like to say.

An entrepreneur who starts a company with his own money is taking the highest risk of anyone involved in business. He may lose his entire capital if the company turns out badly. Yet most Silicon Valley companies are usually not entirely self-funded. Typically the founders put in some capital and sweat equity, but much of the capital comes from others such as angel investors or venture capitalists. That mitigates a large amount of risk.

An employee is even more shielded from risk; he's only risking his labor. While it's painful to watch several years of your work go up in flames when a company goes under, it's hardly the end of the world. Also, in most cases you can tell if the company or product will be successful long

How do venture funds work?

You likely think of venture funds as being like closed-end mutual funds—investors put money in at a given Net Asset Value, and later cash out by selling out their shares to others.

However, since startups are so hard to value and good venture funds aren't a commodity, the model is completely different. First, venture funds are typically only available to accredited investors ($1 million or more in assets). Second, they use the capital call model; investors commit to a certain sum of money, but no money changes hands at that point. Only when an investment is made does the capital call go out, and then the investors have a few days to provide the money.

Finally, you can't just cash out of the fund. As VC-funded startups have liquidity events (buyouts or IPOs), they pass results back to the investors minus fees to the fund managers). For an IPO, the shares owned by the fund get divided up among the investors, so the fund itself doesn't sell the stock. Note that fund expenses are substantial (2% expenses and 20% of any profit isn't unusual), and venture funds have not historically had better returns than other asset classes. However, VCs are fabulously wealthy. An intelligent investor will draw his own conclusions.

One side effect of venture funding is that because funds tend to have a 10 year payout cycle, startups are usually pressured to have a liquidity event within 10 years of being funded.

before spending several years there.

And really, what's the difference between watching your startup fail and having your project get canceled at a big company? Also, you're no more immune to a layoff at a big company than at a small one. At the very least, if you work really hard at a startup and it succeeds, you'll get a commensurate reward (provided you negotiated adequate stock option compensation). It's not unusual to hear stories of people at large companies who've worked very hard, only to get passed over for promotions in favor of those more skilled at office politics.

However, there is one area of risk that might keep you from joining a startup, namely health care. A bankrupt company cannot provide COBRA coverage. If you're young and healthy, you can easily get private insurance if needed. But if you have a chronic disease or have major health-related changes coming, larger companies tend to have better health plans and laid off workers can get COBRA coverage.

Are Startups For You?

In practice, a failing startup usually gives lots of warning before going under, so I'd still accept an offer from a great startup that provides health insurance. Just be extra alert to the possibility of failure, and always keep your resume up-to-date.

Ultimately, how risky a startup is depends more on you than it. Even during recessions, it's not been unusual for good software engineers to get multiple competing job offers. But a mediocre one is at risk no matter who he works for.

4 myths about startups

- **I'll have to work 100 hour weeks and give up my life, wife, and kids.** This is the most common myth about startups. It comes from managers and entrepreneurs bragging about their hard work, and how they worked themselves into divorces while running their startups. In reality, as a startup engineer, you're paid as much for your creativity and problem solving skills as for your ability to just crank out code. 100 hour work weeks don't encourage the former, and I find that after 50-60 hours a week most people start doing unproductive things at work anyway. It's true that since many startups operate in build mode for years, it's not unusual for an engineering team to really jell and do many things together. In big companies, rotations and reassignments prevent teams from becoming this close. A startup's cohesive team can overcome its endemic resource shortages. However, you can end up working at a disorganized startup with such inexperienced founders that you spend all your time at work because you're doing their jobs in addition to yours. In that case, you joined the wrong startup. Those people would have been unbearable to work with even at a big company, and your interview process needs to weed out such startups. Being married is an asset if one of you works at a large company with good benefits while the other works at a riskier startup. The startup employee gets the best of both worlds via coverage from their spouse's large company health benefits.

- **Most startups don't succeed, so my work will be wasted.** 60% of new businesses shut down within four years. Odds are actually a bit better for venture backed Silicon Valley companies. 45% of those either go public or get acquired by a larger company. While some acquisitions don't generate any value for employees, it's still not all that big a risk. After all, at some large companies you could have a major chance of either your project getting cancelled or a layoff.

- **Startups are for young people—kids out of school. They don't want experienced folks like me.** This is a really common belief. In reality, most startups are not well-served by kids out of school. At Escalate,where I was the first employee, Steve Yen and I started off with a system design, and then implemented the system in six months while hiring people. We could do this because we were experienced systems designers who could design a modularized system that made speeding up implementation a matter of adding people. As each new engineer came onboard, he was given a component with an already specified interface to implement. When the entire system had came together, we already had all the pieces together to instrument it, so making performance improvements was exceptionally fast as well.

  Google is famous for hiring fresh graduates. As it turned out, this wasn't a good strategy. An early such employee designed the ClientRPC communications infrastructure. Talk to any experienced Google engineer about ClientRPC and you'll hear horror stories and some not very polite comments. Fortunately, Google became well enough known to attract Jeff Dean and Sanjay Ghemewat, two experienced designers and engineers who replaced ClientRPC with a simpler and easier to use RPC system and protocol buffers. This isn't to say that fresh graduates can't be brilliant engineers, just that an experienced engineer should never discount his or her value to a startup.

- **I'll have to take a pay cut to join a startup**.
  I'm half-convinced that this myth was started by Silicon Valley venture firms to reduce their portfolio companies' recruiting costs. You'll most likely have to take a pay cut if you're starting your own company—that's no different than if you decided to start a McDonald's franchise. However, startups have to pay employees a competitive salary and benefits. There are a lot of Silicon Valley startups at any given time, and there's no reason to take a pay cut except to get more equity. And chances are, companies where you'd

want to take a pay cut to get more equity won't let you do so!

Stages of a startup

People like to classify a startup by how many employees it has. It's a very useful metric, since it does roughly correspond to the startup's business stage. However, hardware startups can differ significantly with respect to headcount at each stage, so I'll name each stage based on the state of the business and give an approximate headcount range. Also, due to their nature, some companies, such as Pure Software when I joined, can be at a more advanced stage than headcount implies. For example, startups bootstrapped by the founders writing code while also working another job can finish the product and sales phases before needing any venture funding.

Idea and conception

Number of Employees: 1-2

At this stage, the company is just the co-founders trying to figure out a product to work on. If they are designers and engineers, this is when they build a prototype to see if the idea has traction. They then use this prototype to help recruit, raise money, and figure out where to go. In many cases, the product is adequate to launch or sell to the general public.

If you receive an offer from a startup at this stage, you should demand high stock option compensation. A key first employee deserves no less than 1% of the company, possibly more to account for future dilution. At this point, you'll possibly have to rely on COBRA for your health insurance, and if the idea doesn't pan out or result in funding, you'll soon be back in the job market.

The funding required to get to this point is usually minimal. Founders can fund it out of savings or work on their ideas while having a day job. Note that it's a bad idea for an engineer to have a day job other than as an independent consultant. There are few Silicon Valley companies that don't require signing away your intellectual property rights while working for them. During the 1995-2001 Internet bubble, many startups skipped this stage due to plentiful funding and it being hard to build an engineering team due to a shortage of available engineers.

Product development

Number of Employees: 2-20

At this stage, the startup is building its product. Its primary emphasis is on engineering and product development. Product development is probably driven by the founders and engineers rather than product managers. This is particularly true of software-driven startups, since a single product manager can generate enough work for 50 engineers. If a company only has about 12 or so engineers, it'd be too easy to overwhelm them. If the product has a long sales cycle, it isn't unusual to start hiring sales people to initiate talks with potential customers.

Offers from startups at this stage should include substantial stock options packages, even for relatively junior employees. You can usually to get a larger stock option package in exchange for a lower salary, since at this stage cash is still a relatively scarce resource. However, you'll be taking on significantly more risk. Double the figures in "Table 3-1. Typical Stock Compensation" on page 52 to arrive at a fair stock compensation value at this stage.

The funding required to get to this point is typical Series A funding as an angel round or through a venture capital syndicate. Typical amounts are around $500,000 to $2 million, depending on the business model, how much money is available, and how quickly the team needs to execute.

Product launch and sales

Number of Employees: 20-200

Here, you've built a product and preferably beta-tested it with customers signed up to buy it. Now, the key issue is generating enough sales to sustain the corporation. A direct-to-consumer product model reduces, but doesn't eliminate, the need for a sales organization. For instance, you may be surprised that Google had a substantial sales force. Even though its self-service advertising systems easily served many small customers, in its early days its major partnership was with Yahoo! and required a classic long-sales-cycle enterprise sell.

This is usually when non-engineer headcount increases dramatically. Engineering is no longer in "build-it-and-they-will-come" mode. It must both maintain the existing product and build the next.

An offer from a startup at this stage should include a fair options package (see "Table 3-1. Typical Stock Compensation" on page 52). It'll be increasingly difficult to get more options in exchange for a smaller salary, but the risk might also be reduced. This would depend on whether the company is profitable or close to it, but remember that a recently profitable company can still be risky.

At this stage, VCs may be spending large sums of money on the company. Depending on market conditions, the startup might go straight for an IPO rather than take additional funding. 3DO, the Trip Hawkins led video game company, did an IPO in 1993, before it even launched its product! Needless to say, in less than ideal market conditions, companies usually try to be profitable or at least have a useful product before attempting an IPO.

This is a startup's most critical phase—most fail here. Some fail because they never reach profitability. Others fail because the nitty-gritty of running a business sinks in at this point; the "fun" part of product development is over. Even profitable startups can go under in this phase because the temptation to grow through acquisition can be overwhelming. A large acquisition can be a very dangerous distraction for employees, leading to lost opportunities or slower long term growth.

Profitability and sustainability

Number of employees: 20 and up

As mentioned before, a bootstrapped firm can be profitable with as few as 20 employees. For most entrepreneurs, a sustainably profitable business is what they've been striving for, preferably one that will grow for many years.

At this stage, most companies try to diversify the product line so as not to be dependent on only one product. This is usually surprisingly hard to do—it took many years for Microsoft to develop Microsoft Office so its revenue rivaled its operating system. It took two product cycles for Xbox to be a viable video game competitor. But it's still not that market's dominant leader, and only became marginally profitable in 2010.

Assuming profitability has been reached at this point, further funding rounds aren't needed. At this stage, an acquisition or an IPO is the usual outcome for a venture funded startup company. That's because venture capitalists want to return capital gains to their investors, and such **liquidity events** provide those gains as well as high profile advertisements for the VCs' success. A bootstrapped startup's owners can IPO or keep the company private, retaining future profits.

In my experience, staying private is extremely rare for technology companies. SAS, the statistical analysis software company, is the only large company I know that's done so. Keeping top engineers in this model is extremely challenging, since they're usually more attracted to venture backed startups and stock options that could make them the next Google-style millionaire. But engineers working for these firms can still expect fair compensation, either by a better lifestyle or higher pay. Note that SAS is over 2000 miles from Silicon Valley, and so doesn't compete for talent in that market!

Offers from a startup at this stage have almost no room for negotiation with respect to stock options. However, the risk will also be reduced. In fact, at this stage, your critical evaluation factor is the potential future market for the company's products. For instance, Google's internal valuation in September 2003 was $1 billion. Since Google grew to be a $100+ billion company by 2007, employees didn't need a substantial options package to become wealthy.

Further reading

Paul Graham's Essays: http://www.paulgraham.com/articles. (http://goo.gl/Qrto)

Founders At Work: Stories of Startups' Early Days. Jessica Livingston. Apress, 2007. (http://goo.gl/uWXP)

The Anatomy of an Entrepreneur. http://www.kauffman.org/uploadedFiles/ ResearchAndPolicy/TheStudyOfEntrepreneurship/Anatomy%20of%20Entre%20 071309_FINAL.pdf This paper contains surprising facts about startup entrepreneurs. Most founders aren't fresh out of graduate school, despite famous examples. (http:// goo.gl/lyHg)

2

Landing That Job

If you've decided you want to work at a startup, you need to get an interview and do well enough to get a job offer. We'll go over some basic interviewing skills. One of the most important things to find out during an interview is if you're a good match for that company.

Your resume

The first step in getting an interview is writing a resume. There're loads of books on how to write one, so this advice is specifically for software engineers:

- When describing your prior jobs, don't just mention what the job was, but what your contribution was. Did you write most of the code? Did you pair program? Did you set up the process? Who did the design?

- Nowadays, recruiters and other non-engineers scan resumes for keywords. While it's OK to include keywords just to get by those screens, make your resume readable by another engineer first! If necessary, put a "Keywords:" line at the bottom of the resume.

- If you took a significant amount of time off from working (anything more than travel after graduation), you may have a gap in your resume. I don't recommend calling it out. One of the cheesiest things I've seen anyone do was putting up a website declaring that while on leave traveling the world, he considered his job to be "taking pictures, and documenting my trip to the fullest extent possible". Unless you did something that can be substantially called a job (joining the Peace Corps, helping wipe out polio, or serving in political office), I'd only refer to a gap if someone asked.

- Be scrupulously honest about your degree and whether you actually got one. Degrees are easy to check, and not having one isn't shameful. For most of my career, I wrote "Dropped out of graduate school" in my resume's Education section. This didn't hurt my employability one bit. However, being caught lying on your resume **will** hurt your employability.

Maintaining your network

Engineers have a reputation for being bad at networking. This is a surprisingly important task, and easier than ever before with the proliferation of social networking websites. Whenever someone you respect leaves your employer, make a note of their personal e-mail and ask them where they're going (they're not allowed to tell you unless you ask, due to nonsolicit clauses). If you think you'd like to work with them again, ask them to keep you in mind in the future. This one step will ensure that, at the very least, those you respect remember who you are.

If a recruiter or company contacts you, take the time to return their calls and understand where they're coming from. This is important since unless you know what the company's about, you can't judge if you'd be willing to leave your current job for it. Even if it's not for you, someone else in your network might be interested and you can do your friend a favor. This kind of quid pro quo enhances your network, ensuring that as new opportunities come up, you'll know about them earlier.

Getting the resume out there

If you're a famous computer scientist, you could probably just put your resume up on a website, write a blog post declaring your availability, and then wait for job offers to roll in. Most of us don't have that stature, so we have to do a bit more work.

Your best bet is with people who know your work. Think of all the folks you've known for the past five years who'd be glad to hear from you. Now get in touch and see what they're up to. In particular, anyone who's left for a startup is someone you must make contact with. In addition, job sites such as HotJobs, Yahoo Jobs, Stack Overflow, etc., are a good place to post your resume.

I got my first job out of school via someone I worked with at Bell Communications Research. At the time, I was an intern and Sudhansu Jain wanted to learn about some basic data structures. I stopped by his office for an hour and gave him a primer, as well as pointers to some recently published papers on the problem he wanted to solve. When he later moved to California and started working at Adaptive Technology Corporation, he met Reed Hastings and told him he should hire me. That led to my very first startup interview.

What startups would you be happy at?

As a software engineer, I find that I'm happiest in companies where software is the primary driving factor in the company's success. I don't rule out hardware startups, but software must be important to the organization. Otherwise, my job will always take a back seat to what the company *does* consider important.

Mirapoint was a mail server appliance company. At that time, it was known in the industry for having the best back-end, but a lackluster front-end. I was offered a job as the manager of the front-end team. Taking the job turned out to be a mistake, since the company did not value front-end work. Instead of emphasizing usability, the testing group focused on testability. As a result, many technologies that could've resulted in a better user experience (such as Javascript) were ruled out in favor of having a plain HTML front-end compatible with every browser on the internet.

This made my job extremely difficult. My team couldn't iterate the UI because releases were tied to back-end schedules. We had to persuade the entire company before we could make any interesting UI change. In the end, when Google came out with an e-mail solution with a great UI, even the best back-end in the industry couldn't save Mirapoint from bankruptcy. This happened despite Google having been one of Mirapoint's customers.

The point of this story is that if your role is incongruent with the company's strengths, you'll have a hard time with your job no matter how good you are. Years later, at Google, I had a conversation with Amit Singh, the manager of the Macintosh software group. He told me about the difficulty of getting resources, since, as a server-oriented company, Google simply wasn't set up to do client software development such as Google Desktop Search. While Google did do GDS, it was harder than it might have been elsewhere. I heard from him echoes of my complaints when I was at Mirapoint.

As a result, when a software engineer asks me if this hot electrical engineering CAD startup would be good for him, my response is almost always; are its stars all electrical engineers? Are there any who're computer scientists? If not, there'll be relatively little respect for computer scientists, and it might not be a good place for you.

Note this doesn't mean the startup wouldn't be lucrative (the right one always is—Silicon Valley is full of stories about administrative assistants who became millionaires overnight because of a hot IPO), but it does mean you could feel unfulfilled unless you are so well compensated that the reduced job satisfaction isn't an issue.

Before you interview

It's important to keep in mind that if you're still currently employed, you're bound by the contract terms of your existing employer. This means you should continue to keep secret any of their secrets. For instance, if you're working on a top-secret feature on the next product, you're under obligation not to disclose it to anyone, whether it's another engineer or a HR person.

If anyone at the prospective employer tries to get you to break that, I'd regard it as a red flag. Someone trying to get you to screw your current employer is very likely to screw you over as well.

In the same vein, I'd be wary interviewing with privately held competitors. The most famous case of this was when Microsoft hired Anders Hejsberg away from Borland, but note that when this happened, both Microsoft and Borland were publicly held companies, and what Hejsberg was working on (Delphi) wasn't a secret. The ethics of interviewing with a privately held company while working at another one in the same product space are much more questionable.

This is particularly true when competing venture capitalists fund different startups to attack the same market, such as when Mpath and TEN (Total Entertainment Network) were both founded to address the on-line gaming market. The competitor might only want to interview you to extract trade secrets or inside information about corporate strategy. It's best to avoid such situations altogether.

Interviewing

There are lots of books and websites on interviewing, but none of them are of any use if you're an engineer. That's because engineers are interviewed by other engineers, who tend not to ask worthless questions such as "Where do you see yourself in five years?". A technical interview has to focus on several areas:

- What do you know? Do you have the required Computer Science knowledge, skills, and tool familiarity needed to do the work?

- Can you learn quickly? When presented with a problem, do you have the ability to attack it with the tools you have at hand? If you get stuck, do you know when to ask for help?

- Team/Culture fit: do you get along with people you don't necessarily agree with?

Nail all three of these aspects and you'll get the job. Let's discuss each of these areas.

Knowledge

Once upon a time, building software was considered a matter of software engineering. Much emphasis was placed on how to break down a problem, split it into pieces, and solve them. Modularity was important, and design skills were emphasized. That's all still important today, but employers now operate in a network universe and face large scale problems. They take those skills for granted (i.e., you're expected to know all of those things). Their interviews focus on the Computer Science knowledge required to design and build internet-scalable systems.

Basic Computer Science knowledge

This is the equivalent of being able to multiply and divide:

- Data Structures and Algorithms. You need to know all of them, when to use one instead of another, their characteristics, and how to implement them. My list of basic data structures include (but isn't restricted to): arrays, linked lists, hash tables, binary trees, balanced binary trees, tries, heaps, graphs, and B-trees. You need to know basic algorithms for sorting (many engineers seem to graduate from school ignorant of heapsort, quicksort, and bucket sort) and searching (binary search, A*). A knowledge of dynamic programming is frequently useful. You should know at least a few heuristics to attack NP-complete problems.

- Programming skills: At the very least, you should know a declarative language (such as Prolog), a functional language (such as SML or Haskell) a procedural programming language (such as Pascal), an object-oriented language (such as Smalltalk), a scripting language (such as Python), and a systems language (such as C). You should have done at least some minor programming in assembly language. If you're a database person, you need to know SQL. This isn't to say you've written major projects in all these languages, but you should know what tools would be useful in what situations, and what you can do. Most of all, you should know one language really well. If an interviewer decides to quiz you on that language you'll be able to answer the question correctly, or be able to reason your way to it.

- Computer Science theory: You should recognize an NP complete problem if an evil interviewer hands you one. You must be able to do orders of growth analysis on algorithms. An understanding of probability, graph theory, Bayesian logic, and basic AI approaches would be useful as well.

- Abstractions: a good understanding of how typical abstractions work, and what layers of abstractions do. Network protocols are a good example to study; what happens when a web browser visits a website is a multi-layered study in design. Not all of it is necessarily good design, and a good interviewer might ask you how to improve certain protocols in order to achieve a certain result.

- Distributed programming: Note that if you're working on limited platforms (phones and other embedded systems), you don't need to know this. You need to know the basics of how distributed programming and data partitioning are used to solve large scale problems. An understanding of various compression algorithms is also useful. In particular, there's an entire class of programming problems which rely on the engineer recognizing how data is distributed and designing software to take advantage of it. For instance, sorting is considered an $O(n \log n)$ problem—except when the data is distributed such that you can use a fixed number of buckets, in which case a linear time algorithm works.

Problem solving

I like to divide problem solving questions into several categories:

- Puzzle questions. These typically rely on an insight on the candidate's part. I dislike these questions, but a surprising number of interviewers rely on them. An example is: you have 10 stacks of coins, but one of them has coins that are 1 gram heavier than the others. You're allowed access to a scale, but it'll work only once before it breaks. How do you figure out which stack the heavy coins come from? The only way to get good at these questions is to do a lot of them. I suggest going to your local library and getting all the books by Martin Gardner. When faced with a series of interviewers who like this type of question, I usually try to annoy them by answering their question before they're done asking it. This only works if you recognize the question. It can also come across as being really arrogant, if not done carefully.

- Computer Science application: This is usually a test to see if you can apply basic computer science facts. One of my favorite questions is to ask when you'd use a binary tree instead of a hash table. Poor candidates tend to reply that binary trees take less memory (false) or are higher performing in some respects. However, the real answer is if you need the sorted results on a regular basis then the binary tree is more useful, otherwise, for random access hash tables are faster.

- Coding & Debugging. When I interview candidates, this is when most get rejected. What surprises me is the number of people who claim (or want) to be software engineers who can't write a simple binary tree traversal, linked list traversal, or hash table lookup. It's imperative that you can implement basic data structures and apply them. One way to brush up is to work through an algorithms textbook's implementation exercises.

- Architecture and Systems Design. The important bit here is understanding how to design clear and useful system interfaces. Unfortunately, experience is the only way to get an intuition for which designs are a good match for the problem and which are not. You can also study examples of successful designs that're in use every day— IMAP, TCP/IP, STL, and the Java Library are all good designs to study. In particular, Joshua Bloch's books on Java design are excellent reading. Some organizations also place an emphasis on object-oriented design and design patterns.

- Fermi Estimation. A number of questions fall into this category, with an example being *How many barbers are there in Chicago?* Attack Fermi questions by starting with a general estimate of the initial size of the subject space (the population of Chicago in this case), and then working through various parameters (such as how long it takes for a barber to give a haircut), and multiplying the various factors. It's important to take a humble approach to this—for instance, if you don't know the population of Chicago, don't make a number up. Ask your interviewer for an estimate. If you can, it's useful to cross check your final answer by taking another approach with different parameters. If the answers match up, then you're more likely to be correct and you'll impress your interviewer with your thorough approach.

Interviewing techniques

When I first came to America, I was surprised at how poorly students took tests. For instance, many students wouldn't read through the entire test before attacking the problems. An experienced test taker maximizes points by doing the easiest problems first, before spending time on the difficult questions. That way, if you lock up on a difficult question, you'd still get points for the easy ones.

You can apply similar test taking techniques to interviews. For instance, typical interview questions will have a linear time solution, and make use of only one of a handful of data structures. If a hash table doesn't work, try something like a tree or a heap. If those don't work, you can start thinking of less commonly used techniques such as dynamic programming. It's very rare that an interviewer will pose a problem that can only be solved by a hash-trie.

Another important aspect of interviewing is that you have to think out loud. This is hard for engineers, since they frequently work alone, but thinking out loud is the only way someone else can assess how you attack a problem and give partial credit if you don't come up with the best answer. For particularly difficult interview questions, it's not unusual for even a partial answer to impress interviewers.

Finally, don't be afraid to ask questions to clarify either the problem being posed or about the company you're interviewing at. Even if you don't especially care about the answer, ask a question and pay attention to how the interviewer answers it. Have they thought about what they want to do? The lack of intellectual curiosity is one more data point that is frequently a strike against a candidate.

If you're afraid that you'll lock up during an interview, prepare some questions ahead of time. For instance, you can almost always ask, "If there's one thing about your work environment you would change, what would it be?"

Note that interviewing is a skill. The more you interview, the better you'll be at it. If you have an important interview coming up, you might schedule a couple of less important interviews before it to get some practice in. Those interviews don't have to be at startups. Big companies with high standards also make good interview training grounds.

A sample interview question

I typically start a technical interview with a coding related brain teaser. An example: "In C++, can an abstract class have a constructor?"

Sometimes, I deliberately frame the question counter-intuitively; "How is an abstract class different from a non-abstract class?" Most candidates reply that an abstract class cannot be directly instantiated. They conclude that there's no point having a constructor in an abstract class. However, the correct answer is that abstract class constructors can still be invoked by derived classes. This question isn't really language specific, as any object-oriented language designer would have to make the same design decision. Even if the candidate isn't familiar with C++, he should be able to work through to the correct answer by first principles.

I then follow up with a problem. My current favorite problem goes like this: Imagine that you have to order a bunch of plane tickets, and all you have are their departures and destinations. For instance, you have 3 tickets, SFO->MUC, ZRH->SFO, and MUC->CDG. The proper itinerary in this case is ZRH->SFO, SFO->MUC, and MUC->CDG. Design and implement a program to order an arbitrary number of tickets into their itinerary, and please discuss the algorithm with me before writing any code.

At this point, really bright candidates start asking about edge cases. For instance, what if the itinerary had a loop in it? Are all airport codes 3 letters? Usually, I respond by telling them to assume that the input always forms a valid itinerary, but they'd get extra credit for detecting incorrect input.

There are many possible solutions to this problem, but the optimal performing one uses two hash tables to index sources and destination to tickets to yield an O(N) solution. Once you have the two indexes, you make one pass through the sources index to find the first ticket, and then a second pass through the destinations index to link up all the tickets to form an itinerary.

If a candidate comes up with a greater than linear time solution, I'll ask them if there's a better solution. In all cases, I ask the candidate what the theoretical best running time for any algorithm to solve this problem would be. The correct answer is that you have to look at each ticket at least once, so you can't do better than $O(N)$ time.

I then stage the coding part of the interview by providing the candidate with function and class prototypes:

```
class Ticket {

    string source;

    string destination;

};


void SortTicketsInPlace(Ticket* tickets[],
int size) {

    // candidate is asked to fill in the

    // details here

}
```

I do this for a few reasons. By writing syntactically correct C++, I encourage candidates (subtly) to also try to write syntactically correct code. While I'm happy to ignore the occasional missing semi-colon, an inability to write syntactically correct code in the candidate's language of choice indicates they haven't written code in a while.

Writing pseudo-code in response to a question posed explicitly in terms of function prototypes usually triggers a red flag and a no-hire from me. Pseudo-code is usually the refuge of the architecture astronaut who can talk a good game but can't code his way out of a paper bag.

Secondly, I deliberately provide a function prototype that forces a "sort-in-place" solution. Good candidates take advantage of this to provide a fast solution that doesn't involve any copying. Mediocre candidates copy the ticket array, sort it, and then copy it back. And poor candidates don't even notice that I asked for an in place sort and either print the ticket order (something that students who've only worked on homework assignments do), or try to return a value in violation of the prototype.

Finally, you'll notice that I deliberately introduced an array of Ticket pointers. Not only is swapping pointers much more efficient than swapping Ticket objects, but the two levels of indirection (arrays are also pointers in C and C++) filters out candidates who don't really know what a pointer is and how it is used.

I then have the candidate write code. This is the long part of the interview, and, depending on the candidate, it can be hard to resist providing hints. Many candidates don't know the STL (Standard Template Library) very well. So rather than have them implement hash tables, I ask them to make up a hash table interface by writing down the prototype or class declaration and then using their prototypes in the code. This gives me an idea of what their design skills are like.

One candidate used Python to attack the problem. Since Python's built-in dictionaries are effectively hash tables, that made the problem almost trivial. This is legitimate, since choosing a tool that makes a problem easy is a great engineering approach that's frequently overlooked. We spent the rest of the interview discussing the actual implementation behind dictionaries in Python.

One important caveat when interviewing candidates that choose a scripting language is to probe deeply to see if they understand the underlying implementation, rather than just having a surface knowledge of the scripting language. A programmer who understands that has a much easier time tuning scripts for performance. This is key for large applications.

If there's a bug when the coding is complete, I try to provide an example and ask the candidate to debug it. This also applies to performance bugs, where the candidate turned an O(N) algorithm into O(N^2) code. The trick there is to look for nested loops. In this case, a nested loop over the tickets array generally means an O(N^2) program.

Really strong candidates blaze through the interview and get everything done in about 20-25 minutes. We then discuss hash table implementations (which can lead into a discussion of data structures), or explore the interface provided by the prototypes I initially provided, turning this question into a design problem. If the candidate is particularly apt, or if

I think I need more data points, I move on to another coding problem that's similar in structure but explores another area of computer science.

I prefer big multi-part questions to sets of unrelated questions. I don't want to make the candidate swap out context. The disadvantage is that if a candidate freezes up early, you can waste an entire interview. If they get stuck, I provide them with hints or partial answers. I have on occasion provided the entire algorithm (in spoken form), then asked for an implementation. Such candidates rarely pass the hiring bar, but at least you know if they're the kind of person who can code up a solution if provided with an algorithm.

Arthur Gleckler once said to me, "My goal in an interview is to prove myself wrong at every stage: if I think the candidate is very smart, I'll try to prove myself wrong by asking a tougher question. If he's doing badly, I'll try to prove myself wrong by asking him a different question to see if he can answer it." I think this is a very reasonable and enlightened approach to interviewing.

If a candidate finished their interview and asked, "How did I do?" they were usually a no-hire. Whether this was because they knew they'd done badly and were hoping the interviewer would reassure them that they didn't do so, or whether it was because true incompetence requires a lack of self-assessment, I don't know.

Team fit

When you interview at a startup, employees try to assess if you'll fit in. You also need to decide if this is a team you'll enjoy working with. For example, if you dislike suits, don't work at a place where everyone wears suits. (This might happen at IBM, but it's very rare in startups.)

In the past, I've made it a point to ride my bicycle, in cycling attire, to an interview and do it that way. My take was that if a startup in its early stages has already decided on dress codes rather than valuing an engineer's capability, then I don't want to work there! Companies tend to get more formal as they get larger and more successful, so if your interviewers frown on your casual attire at this stage it's not a good sign. One startup I joined actually had an engineer yell out, "Hire that guy!" after seeing that I'd gotten to my interview by bicycle.

Landing That Job

To make sure you're really a good fit, ask some questions:

- When your team is designing a new system, how do you hash out the design? You want to find out if there's a formal design process. In particular, if it's mostly informal, is it typically dominated by just a few engineers?

- What happens when you check in a piece of code? You want to see if there's a formal code review/code inspection process. You also want to know if there's a source control system in use at all!

- How many managers are there per engineer? The industry standard is around 6-12 engineers per manager, but high quality startups believe in keeping a low overhead., It's not unusual to have 30 engineers to a single manager. In fact, Google had 1 manager (VP of Engineering Wayne Rosing) for 100 engineers in its early days. This only works if the organization is committed to keeping the quality of its hires high, so not much (if any) supervision is needed.

- If you think of any questions that aren't on this list but should be, please post them onto the e-mail list for discussing the book: http://groups.google.com/group/startup-guide

---

Source control systems

It used to be really easy to tell startups that were technically competent from ones that weren't. The incompetent ones didn't use source control systems. The somewhat competent ones used RCS, CVS, or some variant thereof. Some incompetently gullible places fell for Microsoft's marketing spiel, and used Visual Source Safe. Source Safe's data storage format was such that a single corrupt byte would lose all your data. The competent ones used Perforce, Sun Teamware, or a variant thereof. You'd know to run screaming from any startup that used Rational ClearCase, since it's too heavyweight to use without a full time administrator team, and no startup can afford that!

When it comes to source control systems, having several systems is worse than having one system for everyone. More is not better.

Nowadays, with the proliferation of acceptable source control systems (git, Subversion, Mercurial, and Bitkeeper, just to name a few), it's much harder to use them as a distinguishing factor.

Doing your due diligence

When you first receive your offer, take time to go over the various compensation numbers (see chapter 3), but you also have the opportunity to do due diligence:

- Checking references. You can ask for the references of people you'll be working with. This includes managers, co-founders, and anyone you might report to. Most people don't check references on future peers, but it's a good idea if you want to be extra thorough. When checking references, you can ask questions about management style and willingness to promote from within. Many startups fall over when it comes to internal promotions because the outside candidate always looks more attractive. However, there's no manager on the planet who'll admit to preferring external candidates, so you're reduced to asking if a promotion has ever come from within. If the startup is too new for that to have happened, you can check the managers' track records by asking their references. You should consider asking the reference to provide other references as well, to ensure that you aren't talking to the one person who thinks that your future manager walks on water.

- Research the startup's investors. These may be angel investors, or a venture capital firm. Find out what other companies they've funded. In particular, pay attention to what happened to companies that failed or came close to failing—what did the investors do then?

- Ask how many shares are outstanding. That way, if you get an offer, you can figure out your actual compensation package.

Evaluating a startup

It's very hard to figure out if a startup will be successful. Venture capital portfolios fund about 20 startups in order to get five successful ones and four that will break even. So I frequently tell people to figure out if the job they're going into matches what they want in a job, rather than focus entirely on the company's prospective success.

The biggest sign that a startup will do well is if it is already profitable. This is very rare, but they exist, especially if a company was bootstrapped by the founder rather than being venture funded (Pure Software was one such example). But companies such as Netscape went public even without being profitable, and anyone who was a pre-IPO employee at Netscape would consider Netscape a successful company. If nothing else it changed the world.

You could check if the founders have succeeded with previous companies. But by that rule, you would've avoided Google. One potential red flag might be if the founders are all already independently wealthy. This could indicate that they'd be more likely to want to "shoot the moon" and go for a big IPO rather than selling to another company if that made sense.

I was very impressed when Bret Taylor and Paul Buchheit sold FriendFeed to Facebook. It showed that they were willing to take a big buyout if it was better for the company. Escalate should've IPOed in 2000 once it got a customer, rather than waiting for a big win. The conditions were right, and the market could've changed very quickly and become unfavorable.

If the company has launched a product, ask for sales figures and its growth rate. If the product would be useful globally, ask about the international-ization strategy and how many non-US sales offices they've opened. This lets you calculate the likely future growth rate.

Too late to join a startup?

This question comes up very frequently from people who've interviewed at a startup and now have a job offer. The proper answer is, "It's never too late to join a successful pre-IPO startup, but it's always too early if you join a failing company." Unless you can predict the stock market, there's no easy way to make that decision.

Believe it or not, while trying to recruit engineers for Google 11 months before its IPO, I still had prospective engineers telling me that it was too late to join! At that time, Google was valued at approximately $5 billion. Four years later, it was valued at $100 billion. So someone joining then would have made 20 times their options' price.

In January 2004, Google employee options were priced at $12 a share. Then, a senior engineer could have expected about 4000 options, though Google was occasionally more generous. On February 1st, 2008, the stock price was $515. That's about $2 million in capital gains. You can draw your own conclusions if joining Google in 2004 was too late.

In short, if the company has good prospects, it's never too late to take a job there. In fact, post-IPO employees at Microsoft also made large sums of money with relatively little risk.

I like to value a startup by comparing it to a similar public company. For instance, as of early 2011, Facebook stock was valued on secondmarket. com at $28 a share, or $50 billion for the entire company. A comparable publicly traded company might be Yahoo, then valued at around $21 billion. The internal valuation at Facebook set the stock price at $25 billion. That means someone joining Facebook granted stock at a $25 billion valuation could potentially break even, assuming Facebook did as well as Yahoo!.

Note that there's significant downside risk as well, since there's no guarantee that Facebook would even go public! But there's also a chance that Facebook would do much better than Yahoo!. As the investing mantra goes: **No risk, no reward.**

Fast growth

Some businesses have strong network effects. That is, a company with a head start has a significant advantage over later competitors. For example, after eBay became the dominant auction site, buyers and sellers had no incentive to visit other sites.

Thus, there was a huge advantage to pouring lots of money into Ebay early on, advertising the brand strongly, and hiring enough people to run the site to gain enough market share to keep other companies away. (Note that the network effect behind auctions wasn't enough to keep Amazon from chipping away at Ebay's fixed price selling model, so this advantage could be short term in nature)

Other businesses don't lend themselves to fast growth. For instance, development tools tend to be extremely personal and not subject to network effects. Pouring advertising, capital, and money into Perforce Software wouldn't have shut out alternatives in the source control system market.

Network effects businesses naturally lend themselves to venture funding, while the latter are easily bootstrapped. Pure Software, in the development tools space, tried to grow quickly through acquisitions. In a network effects business, this would've been a big boost. But instead, the acquisitions were made too quickly to identify potential problems. Other companies were formed to build more tools. In the end, Pure Software's acquisition strategy made it unprofitable.

There's no reason businesses that aren't subject to fast growth can't be run profitably and still attract high quality employees by judicious use of cash bonuses rather than stock options. But because such companies rarely go public, there tends not to be any press about people like Chris Seiwald's net worth.

The flip side

After you've joined a startup, you often find yourself on the other side of the table interviewing potential engineering or management candidates. At a startup, I strongly encourage every engineer interviewer to ask coding questions. Coding questions are extremely important to maintaining high hiring standards:

- It's impossible to hide an inability to write code. I've encountered any number of "architects" who could talk a great game about the latest and greatest object-oriented methodology, but blanked when asked to write a simple for loop.

- Coding problems are objective. When someone turns an $O(n)$ solution into $O(n^2)$ code, no one at the hiring committee or roundtable can claim the candidate was better than you thought.

- You hire engineers to write code, especially at startups. Those who write poor code have negative productivity, because everyone else has to fix it. If the engineer needs extra training time, it's an opportunity cost for engineers who do the training.

- If you're interviewing an engineering manager, ask coding questions. You need to make sure that the manager understands technical details well enough to make good decisions. Even if a full-blown coding problem is inappropriate, you need to make sure that the manager is familiar with basic algorithms.

The biggest source of job dissatisfaction comes from having low performing colleagues (who either write bad code or write great code slowly and bottleneck the team). If you're interviewing, it's your responsibility to ensure that those low performers don't make it into your organization.

Luck

Most startup stories gloss over luck's role, which happens in many areas. You could get unlucky with an interviewer who hits all your weak spots (or get lucky and get interviewers who ask you all the puzzle questions you already knew). The startup itself could get lucky—Microsoft was very lucky when Gary Kidall turned down supplying the IBM PC's operating system. Google got lucky when Yahoo! didn't choose to buy the company for a paltry $1 billion.

Note that in both cases, "luck" was from competitors screwing up, rather than necessarily being smarter. Silicon Valley is replete with stories about competitors' stumbles giving startups a lucky break.

Further reading

Connected: The Surprising Power of Social Networks and How They Shape Our Lives. Nicholas A. Christakis and James H. Fowler. Little, Brown and Company, September 28, 2009. (http://goo.gl/5hGX)

Ask the Headhunter: Reinventing the Interview to Win the Job. Nicholas Corcodilos, Plume, 1997. (http://goo.gl/JBy3)

How would you move Mount Fuji? Microsoft's Cult of the Puzzle – How the World's Smartest Company Selects the Most Creative Thinkers. William Poundstone, Little, Brown, and Company 2003. (http://goo.gl/qWli)

The Colossal Book of Short Puzzles and Problems. Martin Gardner, W. W. Norton & Company, 2008. (http://goo.gl/9EC7)

Introduction to Algorithms, Third Edition. Thomas H. Cormen, Charles E. Leiserson, Ronald L. Rivest, and Clifford Stein, The MIT Press, 2009. The classic textbook on algorithms and data structures. Unfortunately, most of the algorithms are presented in pseudocode. If this is your first exposure to the topic, make sure you implement the pseudocode in a real program. Interview candidates who have never done so stand out like a sore thumb. (http://goo.gl/CEgK)

The Luck Factor: The Four Essential Principles. Richard Wiseman, Miramax 2004. It turns out that "lucky" people have a combination of traits that lead them to find opportunities that many others overlook. This book describes some of the factors that contribute to "luck", and demonstrates that you can indeed learn to be lucky. (http://goo.gl/Fkvf)

http://www.careercup.com, Gayle Laakmann. Ex-Googler Gayle Laakman runs a website about interviews and interview questions, including a mock interview as well as a book on the interview process.

3

Negotiating Compensation

Ok, you've found your startup, you've survived the interview process, and you've got an offer. How do you decide if it's fair? What can you negotiate? How should you negotiate?

Reviewing your offer

Generally, startup offers have several components:

- Cash compensation

- Stock compensation, usually in the form of stock options

- Fringe benefits

We'll look at stock compensation first, since it's the most complicated.

Stock compensation

Typically, startups offer stock options to employees (especially engineers, who can't be easily paid by commission). The obvious numbers involved are the number of options, the strike price, and the vesting period. A typical offer specifies the number of options and the vesting period.

The strike price, however, can change between your start date and when your options are priced. Usually, the offer letter contains language like, "I will recommend to the board that you receive 10,000 options to purchase company stock at the prevailing market price." There's nothing suspicious about this—I've never heard of a company that didn't live up to these promises.

The reason is that stock options are officially granted by a company's board, which only meets every month or three. At the first board meeting after your start date, it's very possible a new strike price will be deter-

What are stock options?

A stock option gives you, the option holder, a choice to buy (also called exercise) a particular stock at a pre-set price (called the strike price) at any time in the future prior to the option's expiration date (usually 10 years after the issue date).

If the share price when you exercise is higher than your strike price, then you've made money. These are called "in the money" options. Obviously, you wouldn't exercise if the market price was lower than your strike price since it'd be cheaper to buy shares at the market price. These are called "underwater" options.

Technically, companies issue **call** options (which are options to buy shares at a pre-set price). The inverse of this is the **put** option, an option to sell at a pre-set price. Put options make money if the stock goes down. Since companies want their employees to help the corporation succeed, they don't issue put options to employees.

Options are highly leveraged instruments; that is, it costs relatively little to issue or buy an option, but the profits (or losses) are magnified by each stock price movement.

Instead of issuing stock options, corporations can also issue employees restricted stock (stock that can only be sold after a vesting period), though it's very rare for privately held companies to do this, since options are comparatively highly leveraged.

In 2008, Facebook switched from issuing options to issuing restricted stock units. This could be because companies that exceed 500 shareholders must report earnings like a publicly held company. Facebook settled with the SEC to not have to report publicly, and the switch to restricted stock units could be part of the settlement.

mined that reflects the company's current financial status.

You should think about the following stock compensation variables.

Number of options

This is options compensations' *top line*—it represents your amount of company equity. Many people focus on the absolute number of options they get as though it means something—it doesn't. What matters is the percentage of the company you'll own. So to determine the true value of the offer, you also need to know the number of the company's outstanding shares.

To illustrate this, a friend joined Commerce One back before it did an IPO. She was offered 20,000 options, but the company had so little revenue that, at the IPO, the investment bankers reverse-split the stock so she only had 10,000 options. Six months after the IPO, the stock had gone to $600/share, and the board decided to split the stock 4:1 so now she had 40,000 options at $150/share. What's the difference between 10,000 options at $600/share and 40,000 options at $150 a share? Exactly zero.

Another engineer had two experiences at very different ends of the absolute options number spectrum. One startup told him that they'd recently split the stock because the absolute number of options they were offering was so small compared to other companies, their offers were being turned down. Even though the percentage of company ownership they offered was comparable. He thought they should've kept the number small, and used it as a final hiring test to weed out engineers who didn't understand percentages.

Later, another startup offered him 200,000 options. He said "That's a very big number. Now, what's the number of outstanding shares?" His prospective manager replied "I knew you had enough experience to ask that." It turned out the company had 500,000,000 shares. Note that unless this startup did *very* well before its IPO, it'd certainly do a reverse-split beforehand; investment banks want initial share prices at an IPO to be at least $10, preferably closer to $20 or more.

Typically, the percentage compensation goes something like this:

Negotiating Compensation

Table 3-1. Typical Stock Compensation

Title	Percentage of company
VP of Engineering	0.5% and up
Senior Engineer and above	0.1% and up
Entry-level Engineer	0.05%

CEOs hired on after the company's founding typically get about 1% to 10% of the company. Venture capitalists typically take 20% of the company if they funded the company at an early stage. CEOs and venture capitalists usually have much higher negotiating leverage over a startup, and so get better deals.

Note that these numbers are adjusted by the stage of the startup (and thus the amount of risk you're taking by joining the company) as well as the generosity of the founders and the board. In particular, it is not unheard of for engineers in pre-Series A companies to get 1% or more of

Startup funding rounds

Startup funding rounds are typically labeled as Series A, B, C, D, etc. There might also be pre-Series A rounds of angel or bootstrap financing. If a startup is successful and meeting its goals, each funding round increases the company's capitalization as later investors recognize its current value . A "down-round" is when the company's value has decreased, either because the execution did not pay off as expected, or market conditions have deteriorated between the rounds, such as in 2001.

Should you care what stage the company is at? Yes. The later the stage, the lower the risk that it won't pan out, and hence less stock gets handed out. On the other hand, how much stock gets handed out depends greatly on how much the company needs you, as well as the owners' temperament.

What you should care about is if the company is profitable. A profitable business means a much higher likelihood of a payout. An unprofitable business means that yet another funding round is likely, which will further dilute your share of the company.

the company (Facebook's Dustin Moskovitch reportedly got as much as 6% of the company before it was diluted by subsequent funding rounds).

During the startup boom of 2010-2011, it was not unusual for experienced first engineering hires to get as much as 6-15% of the company. While it's not realistic to expect that from every employer, if you have unique skills or valuable experience, the above table might not apply to you.

Google was very generous to its employees with options. On the other hand, a few weeks after Pure Software's IPO, Reed Hastings told me that his big regret was not spreading more stock around. My advice to founders is to be generous—having motivated employees participate in your success will be something you'll be extremely proud of.

The percentage of the company you own isn't fixed. For instance, as new investors add money to the company, the stock gets diluted. Earlier investors' (and employees') percentage ownership of the company goes down. This is normal. If you feel that you're not getting a fair shake, negotiate for more stock up front, especially if you're getting an offer from an early stage startup.

A study I read indicated that dilution in Silicon Valley is about 1% of a company per year, but, for startups, dilution tends to change dramatically as new money comes in. If the company is successful, the company valuation increases at each funding round, so the dilution is usually not a big deal.

However, hardware startups require huge capital infusions after the design phase is over and they have to fund production. In those cases a big dilution event could precede the product launch. This is one of many reasons why many hardware startups outsource production. It reduces startup costs, thus requiring less capital and dilution of stock. Obviously, if a company's schedule slips or products don't sell as expected, further rounds could be "down-rounds".

Vesting period

The vesting period is the time it takes for you to own all the rights to your stock options. The Silicon Valley period is four years with a one year *cliff*. That means if you leave the company within a year of joining, you forfeit all rights to any options. On your one year anniversary, you get the rights to 25% of your options all at once.

After the first year, the standard is that each month another 1/48th of your original options grant vests. That means if you got 4,800 options and left the job after 3 years, you have the rights to 3,600 of those options. Each month you stayed, between the 12th and 48th months, another 100 options vested.

Note that most option agreements give you a limited period after you leave the company to exercise your options. If you think the company has a good chance of success, don't forget to exercise your options when you leave, if you haven't done so already. It also means that if you really hate your job after 11 months, grit your teeth and stay for another month to get the initial 25% cliff vesting, just in case the company does succeed.

I've occasionally heard of 5 year vesting periods (usually also with 1 year cliffs). These are usually far more common outside Silicon Valley, where the average employee isn't as savvy about stock-options. Rather than granting 25% more stock, they tend to be for the same amount but just take longer to vest. I generally advise against accepting such offers in Silicon Valley unless you're absolutely convinced this company will be extremely successful.

Price

The next obvious variable is the price. Since most startups aren't publicly traded, it's set by the board of directors. The board takes into account several factors, including the revenue (usually meager, but can be substantial at a late stage startup), the product development cycle, partnerships that might be happening, as well as the most important factor, employee morale.

One would think that a big factor in the price would be at what price investors are putting in money (usually venture capitalists, but sometimes big companies, as when Microsoft invested in Facebook at a $15 billion valuation in 2007). After all, every round's lead investor usually sets the valuation of the company. The reality is that the internal valuation (as expressed by the stock option prices that new employees get) is usually set at 1/10th of the price that the previous lead investors got. The reason is that investors typically get preferred stock, while employees get common stock. If the company folds, preferred shares owners get their money back before common stock owners.

No Silicon Valley startup would risk having valuable employees walk out just because they got taken to the cleaners on price. Even in cases when a company did a complete reset by zeroing out early investors' equity and revaluing the company at a lower price, employees usually got new options. Also, in order to retain them, they were somewhat protected from such events. Think such resets never happen to successful companies? Think again—Veritas was an example.

Ultimately, price doesn't matter as much as the amount of equity you got, and besides you can't negotiate over the stock price.

Pre-exercise option

This is now a standard feature of Silicon Valley contracts, and if it's not in your options package you need to negotiate for it. Basically, this lets you exercise your options (even the unvested ones) at the provided strike price as of the day you receive your options.

This matters because of the huge difference between long term capital gains taxes and short term capital gains taxes. Short term capital gains taxes are taxed like income, leading to tax rates of up to 40% on a federal basis, and as much as 50% total for Californians. By contrast, long term capital gains usually get favorable treatment—currently 15%.

The catch is that when you buy the stock, the difference between the current market price and the price you paid is immediately taxed as income. If you join a company and immediately exercise the options before the price goes up, no tax is due, so that's the best time to do it. At an early stage startup, it might make sense to wait since you know that the stock isn't going to go up any time soon.

This is a great tax break, but watch your step. During the 1995-2000 dot-com bubble, folks took extremely high risks to get it. They pre-exercised their options while their company stock was high. After the crash, they couldn't pay their taxes in April.

Again, the solution is to exercise early, before the disparity between the strike price and the market price is high, or, if you're at a risky company whose stock just went to the moon, forget about making that extra 25% and just sell. You don't need to compound your risks.

Negotiating Compensation

The pre-exercise clause works by your buying the stock by exercising some or all of your options, then owning it like any other stockholder. That means that if the company goes under you've lost the money, just like any other investor.

If you leave the company before the options vest, the company has a period of time (usually between 60-90 days) during which it can buy back your stock from any non-vested options (of course, you get to keep the stock from any exercised vested options).

There's an apocryphal story that a well known startup's stock administration department was so disorganized that even though someone only worked there for a year, the company forgot to buy back its stock. The employee got four years of vesting for a year's worth of work!

In any case, you can make the argument that if you don't believe in the

What is AMT?

The USA has two tax systems, the regular income tax system, and the AMT (Alternate Minimum Tax) system. You pay the higher of your taxes under the two tax systems in any given year.

Of the two systems, the AMT system is actually much simpler—there're fewer deductions allowed. For instance, state income taxes aren't deductible under AMT.

AMT started in 1969, after a Washington Post article about 155 people with incomes over $200,000 who'd paid zero taxes by exploiting loopholes in the existing tax code. Rather than fix or eliminate all the loopholes, the government decided to simply enact a secondary tax system that eliminated deductions available under the standard system. The taxpayer had to pay the higher tax of the two systems.

This solved the problem of people paying $0 in federal taxes beautifully, and raised additional revenue. Unfortunately, the AMT system wasn't adjusted for inflation. So, over time, more and more of the middle class (especially those living in high income tax rate states like California) were affected. Since fixing the AMT system would require raising the regular income tax in order to be revenue neutral, it's considered politically unfeasible.

We'll discuss more about AMT in the chapter on tax planning.

startup you're working for, you have no business being there. Conversely, if you do believe in the startup, then exercising the stock makes sense, as the cost of doing so is usually low.

Anti-dilution provisions

This is unfortunately so rare in employee stock options contracts that I've never seen it. With an anti-dilution provision, as the company sells more of itself to later round investors, either you're issued more shares or have the option to purchase more shares to make up for the dilution. Note this is not be the same as term sheet anti-dilution clauses VCs use to protect themselves in the case of a down-round.

Qualified versus non-qualified stock options

Tax law distinguishes between ISO (Incentive Stock Options) and NSO (Non-qualified Stock Options). There are minor tax differences between them, summarized in this table:

Table 3-2. ISO versus NSO

	ISO	NSO
Holding period for long term capital gains	2 years from grant + 1 year after exercise.	1 year after exercise
AMT implications if exercise price is lower than current stock price	Timing-based AMT—you get an AMT tax-credit	Not timing based. All difference is income tax.

Neither option is better, since their tax treatments are only slightly different. However, if a company used to give out ISOs and recently switched to NSOs, you want to immediately exercise your options. It's a signal the company's expecting a liquidity event soon, since the non-qualified options have a favorable tax treatment for employees getting them close to the event.

However, of all the companies I was at when they did their IPO, only Google did this.

AMT implications

When you exercise your stock options, you owe taxes if there's a difference between the strike price and the current market price. For ISOs, all of the tax is AMT tax. So if your AMT tax is lower than your regular income tax, you owe nothing. Conversely, if your AMT tax for that year is higher, you pay the difference, but you get an AMT credit usable in future years to lower your taxes when you do sell your stock at a profit.

For NSO, there's no confusion. Regular income tax is charged on any difference, and your stock cost basis is set at the current market value.

Accelerated vesting (change of control)

This increasingly common in stock option packages, but the amount by which it happens varies dramatically from company to company. So pay particular attention to this clause.

Accelerated vesting is usually an executive protection clause. It's not unusual for some top management executives to lose their jobs when a company gets bought. To ensure they don't scuttle good for shareholder deals, their options automatically vest at an accelerated rate ranging from six months to two years when a buyout happens. Yes, that's two free years of work vested immediately upon the buyout—really sweet, but I don't see it very frequently. Since the general contract for stock option packages isn't any different between executives and rank-and-file, employees get the same benefits by default (other than the number of options!).

While I wouldn't quibble about accelerated vesting as long as there was at least six months of it, I'd try to get it in the stock option agreement. If a big corporation you immensely dislike buys the startup, it'll help you leave an unbearable work environment.

Note that options holders and stockholders can get different treatment in a buyout. This is another reason you want to exercise your options early. Stockholders usually get better treatment including voting rights and early notification of proposed buyouts. Stockholders' votes have to be counted in such proposals, while options holders don't need to be notified since they don't actually own the stock.

Compensation in restricted stock

As of 2008, Facebook stopped handing out stock options in favor of restricted stock units. Restricted stock is easier to value than options—unlike stock options, there's no price point where its value goes to zero unless the company itself goes bankrupt.

Unfortunately, when a startup is at the point where it would rather hand out restricted stock than options, the chance of getting a large stock allocation is reduced. At that point, you need to value the company like any other business. Is it growing? Is the cash flow growing at the same rate? What is the projected value of the startup?

Note that while getting a large share of the company is gratifying, it's much more important that the business ultimately does well. If it does well enough, that makes up for almost every other compensation detail.

Both Cisco and Microsoft, for instance, minted millionaires well after their IPOs. While joining either today as a software engineer might not make you wealthy, joining Apple in 1998 (at its nadir, when they had to receive an investment from Microsoft) turned out to be extremely lucrative.

Different share classes

In recent years, there's been a movement towards having a separate class of shares for the founders. In particular, the venture firm Founders Fund advocates a special "F" class of founders' shares . This is so founders can negotiate away the "F" class privileges in later rounds in exchange for profiting from their corporate holdings earlier. As an employee, I'd look unfavorably upon such maneuvers. This is because if the founder gets rich from a funding round anyway, he might not sell the company at a time when it'd make **all** employees wealthy!

The two failed companies I worked at both had refused the option to either take the company public early or to sell to a larger tech firm. Both founders were already independently wealthy and took more risk to get a bigger score rather than cash out. At such companies, what's good for the founders is not necessarily good for the employees, and you should

---

How do you find out how much stock the company has outstanding?

In understanding stock compensation, it is important you know how much stock the company has issued and what's been authorized (i.e. approved by the board but not yet issued). This lets you know what percentage of the company you'll own.

It's frequently difficult to get the answer out of HR or recruiters, but sometimes engineers already there will answer the question (be wary though, since many engineers consider discussing compensation to be taboo). Sites such as secondmarket.com, if they list the company, provide a prospectus listing the amount of stock outstanding.

Finally, if you have any VC friends, you can call them up and ask. This'd also be a good time to try to get any scuttlebutt about the company.

In particular, if a company's large enough to have revenue and profit, you can compare the current value of the company (stock price multiplied by number of shares) against a comparable public company. For instance, when I joined Google, Jeff Rothschild suggested that I compare Google against Yahoo!, which was already public. Yahoo! at that time was valued at $20 billion, while Google's internal valuation was $1 billion. That gave me an idea of the resulting compensation should Google became as successful as Yahoo!. It turned out that I was wrong—Google far outperformed Yahoo! in the coming years.

---

be very wary of such.

Note that successful entrepreneurs such as Bill Gates, Steve Jobs, and Larry Page and Sergey Brin didn't establish their firms with such preferential shares for the founders. Facebook's Mark Zuckerberg is one exception. Facebook's IPO has been delayed for an unusually long time because of this. Note that rejiggering share structure for the IPO in order to maintain control (which is what Google did) is not the same thing as having a separate share structure so founders can cash out before employees!

Cash compensation

Everyone knows what cash compensation is—salary and cash bonuses. Startups frequently try to get you to take a signing bonus—a one time bonus when you start that you have to pay back if you leave within a year. I usually tell people to ignore signing bonuses in their compensation package. The one-time bonus in lieu of a reduced salary (most experienced engineers take pay cuts when they join startups) doesn't mean anything. Especially if your company uses percentages to compute pay raises—the effect of the salary reduction compounds over many years.

If you're leaving an established company to join a startup, expect them to match your salary and bonuses (or with an explicit pay cut), but don't expect any in-the-money stock compensation to be matched except in the rarest of cases. The value proposition of joining a startup is that you're taking on more risk to get the chance of a higher reward. Expecting the extra reward by owning more of the startup and not having to give up any of your equity compensation from the established company is unrealistic.

If you're joining an already profitable startup, you might consider taking a pay cut in exchange for more stock. This is usually hard to do, since an already profitable company usually wants to use stock equity to make more hires, rather than conserving cash. However, it can be done—just be realistic as to what you can get. A 10% adjustment in trading off stock

Compensating engineers

Many engineers don't really know how to negotiate, and don't do it well. This leads to a large disparity between what they're paid and what they'd get on the open market and allows companies to get away with paying them below market rates. At least until the employee interviews with another company and discovers how underpaid they are.

The resulting backlash usually results in the employee leaving, even if the current employer makes a competitive counter-offer. The best way to avoid this is to pay every one a fair salary in the first place, but most companies like to do a yearly small percentage increase instead of consistently matching salaries to their employees' increase in value.

Google was an exception. Fresh graduates who got promotions frequently saw raises in the 20% range, plus additional stock grants. This kept them at market value, and often cemented their loyalty to the company in a way verbal appreciation doesn't do.

In particular, if you see a colleague having to get a promotion by interviewing and getting a better offer, it's a signal to start shopping for a new job. Your current employer probably isn't treating you any better than it treated your colleague.

and cash is plenty.

Don't forget to ensure that you have sufficient salary to live on. While an eventual IPO might make you rich, that IPO could take quite a bit longer if the stock market crashes. An already profitable startup has no need to do an IPO in unfavorable market conditions.

I don't get excited about profit-sharing bonuses. Until I joined Google, the largest bonus I ever saw at a startup (even profitable ones) was around $2000. Certainly nothing to sniff at, but not worth considering when evaluating your overall compensation package.

Fringe benefits

In 1992, the only real fringe benefits widely available in Silicon Valley were free soft drinks and health insurance. In recent years, they've have undergone a veritable explosion. Here are the ones I consider essential:

- Health insurance. This is a no-brainer—I wouldn't take a job without it. However, if you're married and your spouse has a job that covers your health insurance, waiving this requirement lets you work at early stage startups where it's not available.

- Paid vacation (because everybody needs a break once in a while). The Silicon Valley standard is three weeks. More is great, but many people don't even use that.

Here are the common fringe benefits:

- Term life insurance

- Disability insurance

- Free snacks

- Free drinks

- Flex-time

- 401(k) without matching

Much less common fringe benefits:

- Free meals

- Massage

- Gym

- Paid sabbatical

- Matching 401(k)

- Tuition reimbursement

- Business-class travel

Except for disability insurance (which I'd buy myself if not already covered by an employer), I don't consider any fringe benefits a substantial part of compensation. They can go away at any time. In fact, fringe benefits are often first to go in tough economic times.

Negotiating

There are two steps to negotiations. The first is to figure out what it'd take for you to leave your current job, and the second is to figure out if the offered package exceeds that amount. The best time to negotiate is during the offer process, as you rarely have as much leverage later. Unprofitable startups, especially during the product development phase, rarely hand out huge raises. If the startup becomes profitable, the stock will make you rich, not the raises.

Many people approach negotiation as though it's about bluffing—whoever bluffs best gets the best deal. That's not how I advocate approaching it. I don't enjoy bluffing, and I prefer to negotiate from a position of strength. That means several things; even if you have a job, it's useful to have multiple offers from other companies so you have an idea of your market value. In particular, having multiple competing offers is a must if you want to negotiate.

Once you have multiple offers, you can reveal their value to your preferred employer. I've rarely been indecisive about my favorite company after enough interviews to generate multiple offers.

However, if you're still indecisive at this point, congratulations! Hard choices mean you've gotten excellent offers at likely what the market will bear for your talents! In that case, take your time, put together a spreadsheet detailing the offers, and use it as your decision guide to determine the most interesting job.

If getting multiple offers seems like too much work, all isn't lost. Probably the reason you don't have multiple offers is that you like your current job enough that you wouldn't mind staying there. Thus, you can take a relaxed approach to your negotiation.

In this case, you can signal intent by not changing your plans despite the ongoing negotiations. I once took a two week vacation in such a situation. When I got back, my future employer had discovered the shortage of people with my skills—and raised their offer. In this situation, you're not the desperate one, so take advantage of that.

There are many job sites that recommend you never name a salary figure, claiming it sets your pay scale lower than you might otherwise get. I disagree. The best judge of your worth comes from the market and having a competitive offer (preferably multiple ones). Letting one company, no matter how generous, bid for your employment without others validating that offer doesn't tell you anything about your worth.

Letting the company name its price subjects you to a common psychological trick. The hiring manager first calls you with an initial number, anchoring you to it. A few days later, they make a subsequent higher offer, making you feel like you negotiated a better offer. Checking the market every couple of years is much more effective in ensuring you're getting paid market wages than betting on a guess by any company you work for.

To calibrate your offer, you can ask friends at the company about their offers. However, be aware that someone joining a startup early would (and should) get much more stock than someone joining much later. The tradeoff when joining a startup late is you get much less stock for the lesser risk, not just that the options' exercise price is higher.

The negotiation process

There are three phases during which you will cycle through offers and counter-offers. We'll discuss each of them so you understand what's going on and can proceed accordingly.

The teaser

Your first offer frequently isn't any good. For instance, there might not be a raise compared to your previous offer (if you're an engineer with two years of experience or so, a raise should be substantial), or there might be so little equity that you would not consider switching jobs.

Companies provide teaser offers just in case you're so desperate to leave your current job that you'd do anything, even take a lower offer, in order to extricate yourself from a potentially toxic environment. Chances are, if you're any good, you'll have multiple competing offers, so this shouldn't apply to you.

The appropriate response in this case is to laugh at the offer and tell the company to come back again when they have a more realistic offer. This signals two things: you're aware of your market value, and you're not desperate to leave your current job, or that if you are, you're confident of getting multiple offers.

Facebook, Square, and Twitter (as of this writing) are well-known for writing teaser offers. As a company matures and gets closer to the IPO, the teaser offers usually go away in favor of a more realistic first offer.

Gathering offers

Once you have one offer, no matter how unrealistic it is, feel free to shop your offer to other companies (including the one you're currently at), informing them that you have an offer. This signals that you are serious about potentially leaving your current job, and puts pressure on other companies to provide offers as well. If your initial offer is a teaser, do not disclose it to other companies. If it's a significant raise (20% or more), or you have significant equity in the company for your level, then disclose it so that future offers attempt to better the current offer. If none of the current offers are any good, keep interviewing.

For each new offer that comes in, update other companies about your new offer. Feel free to drop companies that are clearly not in the same league as the others, or aren't responsive. For instance, if you've discovered your preferences for small companies, you can eliminate big companies at this stage.

The end game

You have narrowed down your choices to just the top two or three companies and have a clear idea of what your preferences are. This last stage is meant to get a bump from your most preferred company. If your most preferred company also provided the best offer, then you're done and you might feel like stopping the negotiation at this point. However, frequently your preferred company doesn't provide enough equity or salary.

What you do is to call and talk to the hiring manager or other responsible person, and say: "I would really like to work for you, and prefer you to the other companies. However, the other companies are really providing a better offer, and it would really make it easier for me to justify to my family taking your offer if you could at least match them." If your preferred employer caves and provides you with a satisfactory offer, feel free to sign on the spot. If not, you might want to consider whether they value your services highly enough to pay a premium for it.

Negotiating counter-offers

If you're valued at a current job and then tell your manager that you're leaving, you'll likely get a counter-offer. What's important about these is that you should have a good idea why you're departing. You need to actually address the issues that started you interviewing, not just compensation issues. Most likely, resolving them will cause you to either have to transfer to a different group or department or get a promotion.

Even if your current company capitulates, I'd caution against accepting such counter-offers. Most often, the endemic problems that caused you to interview elsewhere haven't changed, and a year or two down the road you'll find yourself in the same situation.

Negotiating with founders

Early stage startups are a special case: not only is the risk higher, but the opportunity for more equity (or in the case where the other founders are non-technical and you're the only technical founder) is quite high.

However, many engineers are naive about founder's stock and may not negotiate sufficiently well.

- Technical founders are at a premium. There's no shortage of designers or business people, but being able to write code that translates a business need into a product is extremely valuable. There's no reason to be short-changed just because you have less experience.

- All founders should vest stock, rather than each founder having shares right at the beginning. In particular, if you're the technical co-founder, you might discover that the other "co-founders" are twiddling their thumbs while you're cranking hard. The vesting schedule keeps the other founders motivated to help out every way they can. The only exception to the vesting schedule is if a co-founder puts substantial capital into the startup, in which case he's not just a co-founder, but also an investor. Needless to say, a co-founder that's got "skin in the game" is much less likely to abandon the enterprise.

- Avoid 50/50 splits. In the case where there's two of you and you are well-matched, a 50/50 split seems to be a natural choice. The reality, though, is that 50/50 is a very bad choice, as it means both of you have to agree in order to move ahead. In particular, the 50/50 split risks the "hostage" problem, where one person holds up a sale in order to get a higher payment for himself. Gary Erickson in his book, **Raising the Bar**, discusses a situation where he did not wish to sell the company, but his 50/50 partner needed the money for her financial security. As a result, he ended up having to raise $15M by borrowing money at 23% interest in order to buy her out! While Clif bar had a happy ending to this situation, most people are not as happy to take on financial risk as Gary Erickson was.

Negotiation case studies

The next couple of pages detail two real life (but anonymized) case studies of negotiations from 2010. Note that, despite the general economic conditions, Silicon Valley is currently the hottest I've ever seen, so these numbers may not match what would've happened when you read this. Don't use these examples as an idea of what you can get, but rather what you should do when negotiating.

In the following examples, I use the same names for the companies; large company X and startup S.

Case Study: Recent Graduate

Recently Matriculated, a software engineer 18 months out of school, had been promoted since joining large company X. But he sensed his project didn't provide the general visibility that'd put him on the fast track for another quick promotion. Furthermore, he was constantly assigned disruptive and unappreciated system administration work which detracted from his primary responsibilities while not providing any recognition. Frustrated, he asked me if he should apply for a transfer to X's Shanghai office. I told him such a move would have an extremely high opportunity cost, and if he was unhappy, he should begin a job search in Silicon Valley instead.

Four months later, Recently had an offer from company S. It was a privately held but profitable company experiencing rapid growth and widespread visibility. Unfortunately, the initial offer was extremely low. Undaunted, Recently told S to think it over and come up with a more interesting offer while he took an already scheduled vacation. Taking that vacation not only refreshed him, but sent a signal to S that he was happy to stay at his job if their offer wasn't up to par.

Upon his return, S offered to bump up Recently's salary by 10%, and provide restricted stock units worth $450,000 at the current valuation, vested over four years. I advised Recently to show the offer to his current manager to get the wheels rolling. X had been losing employees and Recently's job performance had always been nothing short of spectacular. At the same time, I called one of S's executives telling him how impressed I'd been with Recently when working with him.

X counter-offered with a raise that matched S's offer, and offered $600,000 restricted stock units at the current valuation. S responded with $650,000 of restricted stock units. X responded with $750,000 of restricted stock units. Recently wavered between the two offers and asked me for an analysis. As a publicly held company with more than $150B in market cap, it'd be difficult for X to double over the next four years.

However, as a privately held company under $20B in market cap, S could easily do so. I told Recently that if he cared about money, it was very clear that S's package was far better.

Aftermath: Six months later, S performed a 5:1 stock split and its valuation on secondmarket.com had gone to $50B, almost quadrupling the value of Recently's package. He got to work on high impact projects at S and is happy with his new job. He was so motivated at his new job that he was awarded retention stock packages worth as much as his original offer.

Case Study: Negotiating without a counter-offer

Oscar Oldtimer was a highly ranked engineer at publicly held corporation X. After all his initial options vested, he started interviewing at various companies and got an offer from S. But when he went to his manager at X, a counter-offer wasn't forthcoming.

His approach to negotiating with S was to point out that he'd had multiple refresher grants during his tenure at X, and was walking away from many more years of vesting. S reviewed his offer and raised the size of his stock grant by 30%.

Further reading

http://salary.com, http://glassdoor.com. These websites let you look over salaries for a certain job title in a zip code. This can be misleading, since a "senior software engineer" in one company might not correspond to "senior software engineer" elsewhere, especially if a company has wide salary bands.

Raising the Bar: Integrity and Passion in Life and Business: The Story of Clif Bar & Co. Gary Erickson, Jossey-Bass, 2004. The story behind Clif bar (the energy bar company) and how they backed out from a buyout and decided to stay a privately held company with unique values. Erickson uses the metaphor of a bicycling trip through the Alps to describe how he steers his company. (http://goo.gl/APDDi)

4

At Your Startup

OK, you've signed your offer letter and are starting at your new company. Congratulations! Now what do you do? In this chapter we'll discuss employment contracts and a little bit about how to manage your career.

Your employment contract

Most companies don't give you your employment contract until your first day at work. Many people don't realize that it's negotiable, and often you'll want to negotiate its terms. We'll look at the most important usual clauses.

At-will employment

This is very common in California startups. Theoretically, at-will employment means you can leave a job at any time, and your employer can fire you at any time. In practice, most employers won't risk a wrongful termination lawsuit, and will first put you through a performance improvement plan process. Given that, I wouldn't be overly concerned about this clause. Note that this doesn't apply to acts of gross stupidity, such as getting drunk at a company function and then taking a swing at the director of security in front of the police! That'll get you an exit interview the very next day, after you've spent the night at the local jail!

Non-compete agreement

When Google hired Kai-Fu Li, his then employer Microsoft sued on the basis of his non-compete agreement. This eventually forced Google to pay Kai-Fu Li a year's compensation while he effectively couldn't start work. You rarely hear of such cases in California because non-compete agreements aren't enforceable there. However, since Microsoft was based in Washington state, Google was forced to settle and have him wait out his non-compete period.

Takeaway: don't worry about non-compete agreements in California, but, for all other states, please check your local state statutes and consult with a lawyer before signing such an agreement.

Note that just because California makes it difficult to enforce a non-compete agreement doesn't mean that you can walk out with your existing employer's source code and re-use it at a new employer! Even if you wrote the code, that's stealing intellectual property and can have dire consequences. The classic example was Cadence versus Arcsys, which resulted in Synopsys (which acquired Arcsys) paying $265 million for intellectual property that ex-Cadence employees brought with them when they started Arcsys.

Another common non-compete clause is that you can't sit on the board of directors of any competing companies, or own stock in competing companies. While this may seem perfectly reasonable, it can be taken too far. For instance, large companies such as Microsoft, Google, or Apple can be construed as competing with almost any other company in Silicon Valley. One reasonable solution might be for you to divest yourself of those stocks and buy only index funds.

However, when confronted with this clause at Escalate, I asked the founder to amend it so that I couldn't own stock in competing private companies. This meant I didn't have to sell stock I already owned.

Note that if you have a large portion of your net worth tied up in such stocks and aren't willing to divest yourself, you should disclose that to your new employer during your negotiation period before quitting your current job. Since such ownership can create conflicts of interest between your portfolio and your new job, you and your prospective new employer should work things out before a formal offer is made and accepted.

Non-solicit agreement

Unlike non-competes, non-solicit agreements are fully enforceable in California. A non-solicit prevents you from recruiting from your previous company for your new place of employment, whether or not it's a startup. This is intended to prevent a competitor from recruiting one person, who then guts an entire department by recruiting everyone en masse.

Typically, the non-solicitation period is six months. Sometimes it's as long as a year, but two years is probably excessive. As previously noted though, if someone from your old company contacts you and they ask about your new company, if it has any suitable openings for them, etc., you're free to talk to them about it. Just don't be the first to bring it up.

No moonlighting provision

For salaried positions, there is usually a presumption that you're working all the time for your employer, whether or not you're physically present at the workplace. This is entirely reasonable, since modern workplaces usually allow for telecommuting or flex-time. Obviously, for engineers and other creative positions, ideas can strike at any time, not just when someone is physically at the office.

The no moonlighting provision makes this clear, by requiring you don't take on a second job that may or may not have a conflict with your other job. If you do have a second job as a part-time writer of a blog that generates substantial revenue, or a similar non-competitive position, it's important to mention it and modify the employment contract accordingly.

Intellectual property rights

All Silicon Valley startups require you assign them all rights to patents and other intellectual property developed and invented while employed by the company. Given that engineers are pretty much hired only to develop intellectual property, this is to be expected.

However, many companies take this too far. For instance, most require you to disclose pending patents filed prior to your employment so as to exclude them from the inventions made afterwards. You must take care to disclose these so the company can't claim rights to them. It's not as important if those patent rights are owned by another corporation, since it has presumably taken steps to defend them, but I'd do so anyway.

Also, standard employment contracts state that any work you do using company property is owned by the company. This means that if you do want to start a software-related side business, it's very important you buy your own machines to do that work on, and not utilize, say, the company's internet-access-reimbursement fringe benefit for any work related to the side business.

Google has enforced these property rights clauses on previous employees, so read this clause carefully. If it's particularly onerous, either negotiate with the company, or remember to sever ties with them before pursuing any technical work if you strike off on your own.

Managing your career

While established companies have lots of politics and the need to manage them, startups are blessed with a laser-like focus on one thing:

Make the Company Successful

Nothing else is as important! If the startup is unsuccessful, it doesn't matter whether or not you got the corner office—you'll be evicted from it just as fast as the folks in the cubes. But if it is successful, an early entry-level employee can be as wealthy as a late-joining senior engineer. Unfortunately, this often isn't the case as the early engineer might not have negotiated their stock compensation package as well as a late joining executive.

If you have any success at all as a startup engineer, then the startup will grow. Then you'll frequently have the option to go into management. Frequently, engineers resist and avoid doing this for many reasons:

- Fear they won't get to write code after the transition. This is reinforced by the fear that after a year of not coding they might forget how.

- Fear that they'd be poor managers and leaders.

I've moved between engineering and management at various startups, and I think those fears are overblown. If you have substantial responsibility for managing engineers at all, you'll be faced with technical problems nearly every day. Being able to read code and dive in if necessary makes you a better manager, and since you're an engineer yourself, ones on your team will pay more attention to you.

As far as your being a good manager is concerned, I think the bigger concern should be:

If you don't take on a management job, the company will have to hire a manager from outside, and he or she could be far worse than you'd be.

In my career in Silicon Valley, the only company where I routinely met better managers than I would've been was Google. It was obvious that Google had great managers, but even there I eventually learned that my career prospects would've been far better as a manager than as an engineer whose responsibilities included management-type work.

As an engineer, you won't get credit for any of the management-related work you do, but as a manager, people are impressed you can code. Which would you rather be?

You might not be cut out to be a great manager, but if you don't try, you've no way of finding out. If it turns out you dislike management, it's easy to back out of it. If the company hires a bozo to manage you, getting that manager fired is difficult.

Most people associate being a manager with having an MBA. However, most engineering management jobs, especially at the technical lead/first level manager level, don't involve MBA type tasks like ROI computations or Net Present Value analysis. Management at that level doesn't require anywhere close to the amount of study it took you to become a half-way decent programmer.

That's because management is a soft skill, not a math-requiring science.

At Your Startup

Thus, a handful of management books should be all you need to become a good manager. It's useful to read them even if you're not a manager, so you learn to recognize good management and leadership, as well as poor management so you can avoid it.

If you intend to become a manager, realize that companies frequently use the tech lead or team lead position as a stepping stone to management. It's imperative to demonstrate that you have leadership ability even if the team doesn't need a full manager at the moment. Startups can grow rapidly and it's dangerous to assume that your team won't ever need a manager. If you're proven right, then your decision to work for that startup was a mistake!

Successful Silicon Valley startups are run by engineers, not MBAs. HP was very successful when both founders (Bill Hewlett and Dave Packard) were in charge. Similarly, SGI and Microsoft were most successful when their engineering-oriented founders were at the helm. They notably stumbled when the reins were handed over to MBAs and other "professional" managers.

Right from the start, when he founded Pure Software, Reed Hastings was a great manager. It wasn't until professional managers showed up that Pure became a much less fun place to work. Similarly, Wayne Rosing said that Google was much more fun and made better strategic decisions than Sun Microsystems did because Google had more engineers in senior management.

In the book *Built to Last*, Collins and Porras observed that successful companies tended not to hire CEOs from outside the company, but promoted from within as much as possible. They built a "deep bench" of strong managers steeped in the corporate culture. It's important that engineers step up into these roles as much as possible.

Outside managers, no matter their credentials, frequently bring cultural baggage that doesn't apply to a startup, and often do more damage than hiring internal managers does. It's easier to learn the mechanics of management than it is to cultivate and preserve a company's culture.

Have no respect for job boundaries

If you're used to a large company where everyone has a different, specialized, role, a startup's lack of job boundaries will bother you. You might act as an engineer one day, a sales person at a conference the next day, and a recruiter at a school job fair a few days later.

This is part and parcel of being at a startup, and you should enjoy it while it lasts. As the company grows, these opportunities have a way of slowly disappearing or becoming less important than specializing in a job. The ability to impact many areas of the organization is one reason I've repeatedly worked at startups.

Management structures

Most Silicon Valley startups I worked at used the traditional hierarchical command-and-control structure similar to the military's; a CEO at the top, and then a tree of managers down to the individual contributor level.

There's much to be said for this. Decisions and large scale changes can be implemented quickly. Leaders and managers can be measured and judged on how their teams perform, including who they hire. Teams tend to be more cohesive and stay together long enough to gel, because good leaders attract strong teams who want to stay together because of the trust level that's been built up. Reed Hastings recently told me that he's still the biggest fan of "the traditional management model executed excellently."

The downside is that this model is hard to do well. It's very difficult to hire and train great leaders and managers. I've worked with truly great managers, but the awful ones really left a bad impression. If you hire a bad VP of Engineering or a really poor director, it doesn't matter how good the CEO is.

One VP I had didn't walk around and talk to individual engineers for six months after an initial one-on-one with each engineer, even though the startup was a 25 engineer company! Another director I encountered would walk into an engineering meeting to ask our opinions about the room's decor. That lack of respect for engineers led to a dramatic loss of morale, and subsequent departure of talent.

Google took a very different approach. It started off with a flat hierarchy. At one point, Wayne Rosing had all 100 engineers reporting directly to him. This precluded doing one-on-ones every week, but it worked be-

At Your Startup

cause Google hired very high quality engineers who could be pointed at a problem and left alone to solve it. Since good engineers enjoy that sort of autonomy (and those who didn't very quickly left; the culture almost always rejected them right away), this made them even more determined to justify that trust.

During an engineering meeting, Wayne Rosing once said:

> "When I was at Sun, after a few years, I realized that all the people doing real work were six levels away from me, all the way at the bottom of the management structure, and I had managers whose goal in life was to become directors, and directors whose goal in life was to become a VP. I decided at Google that I wanted to get away from that as much as possible. Management at Google will be the toughest management job in the Valley: we will give you so many reports that you cannot possibly micro-manage anyone reporting to you. We will take away your hiring and firing decisions and put them at arm's length, so you can't bring in your cronies to work for you. Management at Google will be much more about leadership than managing."

When I joined Google in 2003, I was very impressed by how well this all worked and scaled. While I'd met truly good managers before, Google had engineering directors that were amazingly good at leadership, rather than people interested in control. When I showed Wayne a preview of this book, he wrote:

> "I believe there was at least another factor of 10 left in the hyper-flat structure. But the keys are very basic: avoid non-engineers in management of engineering, give people creative and intellectual freedom but in a constrained way (hence the 20% time memo) in terms of productivity impact. Preserve a hot young computer science department-like atmosphere with respect for integrity and truth. And last, keep the ratio of engineers to others in balance; Maximize your expenditure on people who create the wealth, not those who take a cut of it."

Where Google fell down was not giving hiring the importance it deserved with respect to what engineers were asked to do. Interviewing was a major burden; each 45 minute interview was really an hour and a half of work to prepare for and write up. Most interviews were fruitless since it took many candidates to hire one good engineer.

However, interviews were viewed as a form of community service and not really "work". That was fine when I joined, as existing engineers were usually enthusiastic about getting great people, and the hiring committees were highly motivated to keep engineering as strong as possible.

However, in 2004 hiring was ramped up in a big way. This meant hiring committees were split up to process the hiring load. Standards started to drift between the various committees as they didn't have a way to sync them up. Even more importantly, some committees had to meet twice as often to handle the load. At one point, hiring committees and interviews took up 25% of my workload. Since it wasn't considered real work, I was at a disadvantage during the peer-based promotion cycle.

By late 2005, many senior engineers (myself included) quit helping hiring in order to protect their bonuses and promotion chances, resulting in a decline in hiring standards. The nadir came when someone on a performance improvement plan (in other words, about to be fired) regularly showed up at a hiring committee, giving feedback and helping decide who'd be hired!

I was recalled to a hiring committee in 2007 after several low performers had been traced to 2006's hiring mistakes. Google had essentially dismantled all the site reliability engineering hiring committees except for this reconstituted one.

Unfortunately, Google didn't fix the root cause. A peer-based model performs very badly once you've done a number of poor hires. Once gaming the system becomes a short cut to getting promoted, that quickly becomes the dominant strategy, with engineers who aren't gaming the system shoved aside by those who've learned how.

Regardless of this flaw, I think most startups would do better by trying a peer-based model, since they must have excellent hiring controls anyway. Speaking as an engineer, the autonomy provided by a low control/high trust model is much more satisfying and motivating, but the career support and learning provided in a well-done command-and-control model is more thorough.

At Your Startup

In any case, I don't think a company's management structure should be a factor in selecting a startup, since in both structures execution is everything. It's possible to do traditional management well and badly, and the peer-based model can easily turn out to be just as big of a disaster. I don't think it's a coincidence that Google's peer-based model started falling apart after Wayne Rosing retired.

Stock option refreshes

Many startups don't automatically provide refresher stock grants as part of compensation. I think this is a mistake, because valued employees tend to start looking elsewhere as they approach the end of the four year vesting period. Google had a policy of issuing stock grants to valued employees after two years. Then refresher options were granted every year. This sealed employee loyalty, and, after several refreshes, makes it very hard for other companies to hire away employees with such **golden handcuffs**.

Further reading

Peopleware: Productive Projects and Teams. Tom DeMarco and Timothy Lister, Dorset House Publish Company, Inc. 1999. This is the must read book for team leads and managers. Its authors are humble enough to tell you that they don't know how to get a team to gel, and then provide several examples of how teams are prevented from gelling. If I was a CEO or VP of Engineering, I'd make everyone read this book, whether they were an individual contributor or in management. (http://goo.gl/X3hw)

Built to Last: Successful Habits of Visionary Companies. Jim Collins and Jerry Porras, Harper Business, 2004. The classic book on how to build a strong corporate culture. (http://goo.gl/TraD)

How the Mighty Fall: And Why Some Companies Never Give In. Jim Collins, Jim Collins, 2009. This is the book that gives the lie to the typical myths about how companies fail. Collins shows that it isn't lack of innovation that causes failure, but hubris and excessive confidence. (http://goo.gl/qY1C)

The Fifth Discipline: The Art & Practice of The Learning Organization. Peter M. Senge, Broadway Business, 2006. An excellent book about how an organization's structure affects its performance, no matter the quality of its individuals. (http://goo.gl/zxJd)

Drive: The surprising truth about what motivates us. Daniel H. Pink, Riverhead Hardcover, 2009. The book isn't as good as Dan Pink's talk about the topic (http://

www.ted.com/talks/dan_pink_on_motivation.html). We understand much about how incentives do or do not help performance, but don't know how to apply that knowledge to large organizations. (http://goo.gl/Ltdg) (**Video is at:** http://goo.gl/XnQU)

Startup Engineering Management. Piaw Na, Piaw Na Publishing 2011. I wrote a book about managing engineers in a startup environment to cover many topics I touched upon in this chapter in greater detail. (http://books.piaw.net/management/index.html)

5

Tax Planning

Joining a small, private company that offers stock options means you need to do tax planning unique to that situation. Note that the following advice **only** applies to **privately held** startups and doesn't apply if you're at an already public company.

Exercising your stock options

As mentioned in the chapter on negotiating compensation (see page 49), I recommend exercising a year's worth of options as soon as you can. This does several things:

1. You're now a stockholder, not just an employee. The company's required to notify you of substantial changes to its structure, whether it be an acquisition, a new round of funding, or liquidation.

2. Most importantly, it starts the clock on the long term capital gains period. If the company's successful, your profit from selling exercised options will be taxed at the favorable long term capital gains rate, instead of as income. This is particularly important for cash acquisitions. As far as they're concerned, you've no choice as to when you dispose of your stock—it happens even if you wouldn't have wanted to sell. In this case, the earlier you exercise your options, the more likely your gains will be treated as long term capital gains.

3. If the startup's acquired, you may have rights that options holders don't have. For instance, you get to vote on the acquisition, and you're entitled to any cash payments. Options holders don't automatically get them.

4. If you leave before your four years of vesting finish, there's a slight chance that your company's stock administration department forgets to buy back the stock at the exercise price. If this happens to you, please write me, since I've never found a documented case of this happening.

5. If your company's successful, you may qualify for Section 1045 stock rollover rules, letting you invest your profits in new startups without having to pay taxes. If you wait until the company's been capitalized at more than $50 million to exercise, you won't qualify for this.

6. You may qualify for the Section 1202 capital gains exclusion rule, which could save you some capital gains tax. This requires a five year holding period, so the sooner you exercise, the sooner you qualify for this rule.

If you can't exercise even a year's worth of options because you can't afford to take the risk (your strike price could be very high because the company is about to go public), exercising even one share at least makes you a stockholder. That way you'll get regular notifications of any changes about to be made to the company's charter.

Example: Louis Reasoner joined ABC corporation in 2007, after a second round of funding. He received 10,000 options at $5 a share for a company valued at $200 million. He decided to exercise 2,500 options right away and become a stockholder, but he neglected to exercise the rest. Exercising those options cost him $12,500.

In 2009, ABC went public and is now valued at $500 million (or $12.50 per share). Louis decided to sell 5,000 shares. The first 2,500 shares were from his exercised options. Those shares sold for $37,500, with a net capital gain of $25,000. Because these shares were held for 2 years, they qualified as long term capital gains, meaning that he only has to pay $3,750 in federal taxes.

The second 2,500 shares came out of his unexercised options. By using a cash-

less exercise method, he made a $25,000 profit. But, because these gains are treated as income, he has to pay regular income taxes on them. ABC's stock administration department will probably withhold 28% for federal taxes or $7,000. Because he didn't pre-exercise all his options, he'll pay $3,250 more in taxes.

The mechanics of stock option exercise

When you exercise stock options at a startup, what you're really doing is getting restricted stock in the company. The default restricted stock treatment is that you don't report income when you receive restricted stock, but you do have to report income as it vests.

This isn't a good thing. First, at a successful startup the stock will go up (possibly rapidly) over time. Second, after the initial cliff, you'll get stock every month, making reporting and tracking it hell on your accountant, if not on you and your stock administration department.

You get around this by making an *83b election*. This means you treat the taxable event up front—you owe any (and all) taxes due as though all the stock vested the day you exercised. Clearly, if you exercise options immediately upon getting them, you have no tax liability. The difference between your exercise price and the market price is $0.

What if you forgot to exercise your options right away? It's not too late as long as the company hasn't gone public yet. By using an 83b election, you'll owe taxes on the difference between the current stock price and the exercise price.

How to make an 83b election

Your company should help you with this but, just in case you can't get help, here's what you need to do. On a piece of paper, write at the top: "Section 83b Election". Then write the following, substituting your name, your company's name, address, social security number, date of exercise, fair market value, and price paid as required:

The taxpayer hereby elects under Section 83b as follows.

Stuart StartupMaven, 1600 Amphitheater Parkway, Mountain

View, CA 94043, Social Security #: 123-456-7890

Property: 10,000 shares of ABC corporation restricted stock (as per corporation charter)

Date of exercise: 1/1/2003

Fair market value at the time: $10,000

Price paid: $10,000

I have provided copies of this statement as required in the regulation.

Within 30 days after receiving the stock, send the election to the IRS office (the same address you use to file your 1040 tax return). Provide a copy to your employer. If you're gifting this stock, which might be wise thing if you expect the company to become valuable, you'll also need to provide a copy of the election to the giftee.

You must also attach a copy of this election when you file that year's income tax.

If you have a living trust, you might consider exercising the stock under its name. This provides a measure of privacy should insider stock sales by employees have to be made public after the IPO.

When Google went public, it allowed employees who'd already vested stock to sell some during the post-IPO blackout period. Unfortunately, since these were considered insider sales, employees had to file with the SEC. Since the maximum sale was 5% of their total stock options package, and most employees (who now had a huge amount of their net worth tied up with Google) chose to sell all 5%, their total amount of Google stock (and hence their net worth) was effectively visible in finance.yahoo.com's insider trading section.

This understandably upset a few employees (who shouldn't have been surprised—but were used to thinking about C++, not financial reporting). If they'd transferred their stock holdings to arbitrarily named living trusts, their names wouldn't have been public record. As it was, I and others learned the approximate net worth of several co-workers.

Late exercise for incentive stock options

For incentive stock options (ISO), this income is imputed to AMT (Alternative Minimum Tax), meaning for those in lower-income brackets (total AMT income less than $160,000, as of 2011[1]), it's still not a taxable event. Even if you do get hit by AMT, part or all of the AMT liability can be used as an AMT credit in future years. This effectively means that you're not paying more taxes, but instead are paying a portion of the taxes ahead of time (i.e. the difference between the exercise price and the stock price when the option was exercised).

Furthermore, for AMT purposes, the cost basis of your acquired stock is now set at the market price when you exercised! In the (happy) event that the company's stock become valued at a sufficiently large multiple that selling the stock would move you into AMT, this'll reduce the AMT amount you'll owe.

Example: Stuart StartupMaven joined XYZ corporation in 2003, when the stock was valued at $1/share, and was awarded 10,000 incentive stock options. Unfortunately, he didn't have the means to immediately exercise his options.

In September 2009, he had a disagreement with his manager and left the company, just before XYZ did its IPO. Since his options expired within 60 days of his leaving, he had to exercise his options and pay $10,000. Unfortunately, XYZ went public before he exercised, so the stock was at $20/share. To add insult to injury, since these options gave him restricted stock subject to the post-IPO insider sales blackout period, he couldn't immediately sell the exercised stock!

Since he had incentive stock options, the $19 per share difference was now immediately taxable at the 28% AMT rate. Because Stuart quit in September, he had 8 months of his $120,000 a year salary, in addition to the $190,000 in AMT income for a grand total of $310,000 AMT income.

Stuart's federal tax for the year (without exercising his ISOs) would've been $16,067.73. His California tax liability would've been $6,829.07. How-

---

1   As of this writing, there is no AMT patch for 2012, which means that many more people could be affected by AMT in 2012 unless Congress takes action.

ever, because of his stock option exercise, his federal taxes were $73,549, and his California taxes were $25,073.07. Since Stuart didn't exercise his stock options when they were at $1/share, he owed $75,725.27 more in taxes.

This is even though all he did was exercise his stock options—he didn't get a single extra dollar during the exercise period. In fact, he was out $10,000.

In practice, the difference would've been even more, since Stuart, as an imaginary person, doesn't have dividends or other capital gains from his taxable portfolio. However, these additional taxes are an AMT tax credit he can apply in future years if he sells XYZ's stock at a profit. In fact, when he does sell XYZ's stock, he can calculate his cost basis at $19 per share, instead of $1/share. Note that if the stock goes down, he'll be in a world of hurt.

Since XYZ's lock up period expires in April, Stuart has a chance to sell his stock just before he has to pay taxes on his unrealized gains.

The above example is contrived, but very possible. I fell prey to this rule when I left Pure Software a month after its September 1995 IPO. I experienced the agony of paying real money taxes on "paper" gains.

A company's lockup period is usually for six months after its IPO. During that period, departing employees usually have a 60 or 90 day period to exercise their (potentially valuable) stock options but can't sell the resulting restricted stock.

They're in a very undesirable and dangerous situation. First, they're liable for the taxes due on their exercised stock options, but can't sell their stock to pay them. Second, if the price drops so they can't pay the taxes by selling the stock, they'll have to use other assets to pay.

For tax planning purposes, spreadsheets at http://www.taxvisor.com are useful for running hypothetical scenarios for tax planning purposes. Since AMT affects total income taxes in a non-intuitive fashion, you should use Tax Visor in January, or whenever you exercise or sell stock.

Late exercise for non-qualified stock options

The tax treatment for non-qualified stock options (NSO) is virtually identical to incentive stock options. The difference is with an NSO, the entire amount between strike price and market price at the time of exercise is considered income, rather than AMT income. Any AMT you owe won't provide a future AMT credit. However, the elevated cost basis for future sale still holds.

Note that if, as recommended, you immediately exercise stock options when you receive them, exercising either NSOs or ISOs doesn't affect your taxes .

However, when determining if you qualify for long term capital gains, ISOs have an additional holding period. The ISOs must have been issued 2 years prior to sale and held for a year prior to the sale, while for NSOs, the holding period is only one year.

Why do companies mostly issue ISOs? A typical startup has a very stable stock price for its first few years while building the product. If you own a substantial portion of the startup, it makes sense to wait a bit before exercising all of it. Since ISOs get favorable tax treatment, they maximize the amount of time big shareholder employees have to exercise all their options.

A company that's aware of this issue and cares about its employees will switch from issuing ISOs to NSOs prior to making preparations to go public. This is why if your company switches (or did so before you joined), it's a signal to immediately exercise your stock options. I don't know any other reason to make this switch.

Inapplicable situations

Note that you should **not** pre-exercise options if you work at a publicly held company. That's because your options price is fixed when you join, while the company's stock price fluctuates with the market. If its stock price drops below your strike price, you incur no taxes by pre-exercising your options but it'd be cheaper just to buy the stock in the open market.

Conversely, if the stock price goes above your strike price and you exercise and hold rather than selling right away, then you owe taxes immediately and will have to come up with the funds from your savings. Any tax advantages such as getting the long term capital gains tax rate only accrue from the open market price, not from your strike price. So, again, you would've been better off just buying in the open market and holding the stock for a year and a day to get the long term gains rate, rather than pre-exercising.

Once the company is public, pre-exercising your stock-options is a **stupid** thing to do unless you have no other choice.

Example: Sue Timing joined ABC corporation in 2009, and was granted 1,000 NSOs at a strike price of $12.50 a share. After a month, the stock price doubled to $25. If she pre-exercised all her options at this point, she couldn't sell her stock since it was unvested, but she'd immediately be on the hook for $12,500 of income.

If, a year later when her first 250 shares vested, the stock dropped to $6 a share, she would've taken a loss on her exercise, and owed taxes on her $12,500 gain at the time of exercise. If she'd wanted to take on more risk by owning more ABC stock, she could've bought it when she joined, and not be on the hook for the taxes (though losing capital would still be unavoidable). Furthermore, if she exercised all 1,000 options and then left the company after a year when the stock price was below her strike price, the company is under no obligation to buy it back!

Gifting company stock

If you've joined a successful startup, one of the best things you can do is gift stock, rather than cash, to family. This has two advantages:

1. You can only give up to $13,000 a year (in any form) to someone else before incurring gift taxes. You can get around this limit by giving stock currently worth $13,000 that's likely to appreciate and could be worth much more when sold.

2. If you have family members in a lower tax bracket, their stock sale will be taxed at a much lower rate than yours, also making the effective gift larger.

You gift someone stock by exercising your options and effecting a transfer to the giftee. Don't forget to give them a copy of your 83b election so they can file it with their tax return.

What to do if your company fails

Most startups don't just declare bankruptcy and then liquidate. Usually, the residual value of the company (patents, infrastructure, etc) is acquired for pennies on the dollar. At that point, you write off any investments you made in the company as a capital loss.

You can use this capital loss on your taxes to offset any capital gains. If you don't have any capital gains that year, or they add up to less than your capital losses and you've owned the stock for more than a year and a day, you can use it to offset up to $3,000 of income. As long at the total offsets add up to less than the capital loss, each following year you can apply the remainder of the loss to that year's gains and/or do another up to $3,000 income offset.

Hopefully, you would've detected problems in time to polish your resume and find another job. But if not, it's typical for company buyers to employ the existing engineers to try to keep the assets current. If this happens to your startup, then by all means negotiate a new compensation package. Regardless, I'd keep an eye out for new and better opportunities. It's very rare for scavengers to make a success out of a failed startup.

What to do if you do hit the jackpot

Most successful exits don't provide a life-changing amount of money for employees. I came away from my first two IPOs with enough money to put a down payment on a house and purchase a car, but family members were fond of telling me that I would've made even more money if I'd joined Microsoft in 1992.

Successful exits for a startup come in two forms, an acquisition (either in cash or in stock) or an initial public offering. Here's what happens when a company is sold:

1. A change of control immediately triggers any accelerated vesting clauses. This could mean as much as six months free stock for employees, strengthening their position when it comes to renego-

tiating compensation.

2. A stock for stock acquisition grants most of an IPO's advantages without any of the drawbacks. There aren't any blackout periods, and you have the option of holding the stock to get long term capital gains treatment. However, you might not qualify for Section 1045 or Section 1202 treatment.

3. A cash for stock acquisition is effectively treated as a sale of the company on the open market. As such, you're treated as having sold the company on the date of the acquisition. If you don't qualify for long term capital gains as of that date, all gains will be taxed as income.

What is an IPO?

An Initial Public Offering (IPO) is the initial sale of stock to members of the public on a major stock exchange (NYSE or NASDAQ). While many employees and investors view the IPO as the major liquidity event allowing them to cash out their hard earned money (or sweat equity), the IPO's true purpose is to raise cash for the company.

If that's true, then why do most corporations try to achieve profitability before an IPO? The answer is that corporations have to file all their finances with the Securities and Exchange Commission (SEC) before they can sell stock to the public. That means meeting all the accounting standards and becoming subject to regulation. As a result, running the company becomes a heavyweight operation, so only corporations large enough to have all that machinery in place anyway would file for an IPO.

In fact, in April 2004 Google was forced to file with the SEC despite not having applied for an IPO, because it had more than 500 shareholders. As a profitable company, Google didn't need to raise cash, and only did an IPO after their forced filing.

3DO and General Magic were startups that filed for IPOs despite not even having products They were so hyped up in the media that investors were willing to risk money without the companies having any earnings.

An IPO, of course, makes news in the way an acquisition doesn't. But bear in mind that IPOs come with certain disadvantages:

1. There's usually a blackout period, typically six months, when employees aren't allowed to sell stock. If the company was substan-

tially over-subscribed during the IPO, exceptions may occasionally be made. Google, for instance, allowed employees to sell 5% of their stock 30 days after the offering, and 10% after 60 days. Netscape employees were also allowed an exception during their blackout period. Note that these were exceptional companies during exceptional times. Neither Pure Software nor Mpath Interactive allowed employees to trade during the blackout periods.

2. The IRS can investigate companies for issuing stock options prior to the IPO that were substantially below market value. This happens because the reduced stock option price is a good way to recruit and reward valued employees, and is typically difficult to prove. Google was investigated for this, and came to a settlement with the IRS that essentially forced employees issued the "unfairly low priced" stock options to come under Section 409A timing restrictions. Note that this settlement didn't affect those who'd pre-exercised their options, so consider this another argument for early exercising.

As you can see, most of an IPO's advantages are timing related. In particular, being able to control when you sell your stock lets you take advantage of tax benefits such as long term capital tax rates. Two other little known advantages that might accrue to you are Section 1045 and Section 1202 treatments of capital gains.

Section 1045: An investor in a qualified small business who's held the stock for more than six months can elect to roll over capital gains from its sale if another small business stock is bought within 60 days.

This means if you buy stock in a company when it was a small business (defined as less than $50 million capitalization), and it's successful, you can sell the stock (in what's no longer a small business), and use the proceeds to fund another small business within 60 days without having to pay federal **or** California capital gains tax.

There's a caveat that the new business cannot have more than 20% of its payroll outside California—something that most startups have no problems conforming to. Once you've been in a startup, you have an incentive to fund further California startups, one reason other regions have a hard time competing with Silicon Valley for startups.

Tax Planning

You can also use 1045 qualified proceeds to exercise stock options at your next startup. The timing is tricky, since you have only 60 days after you sell **before** you must rollover the capital. Otherwise, you lose the tax advantages.

Example: *Ben Bitdiddle worked for ABC Corporation in 2005 when it was a small company of 20 employees. Back then, it was capitalized with $2 million in venture funding with a post-money valuation of $5 million. Ben had faith in the company and its founders and exercised $50,000 worth of stock options. Fast forward five years, and ABC is now an industry behemoth, with a $500 million market capitalization. If Ben sells $2 million worth of his now $5 million of ABC Corporation stock to found a startup (or to exercise stock options in a startup he joins), all those gains are rolled over and Ben doesn't pay any capital gains whatsoever.*

Section 1202: Up to 50% of the capital gains from the disposal of small company stock can be excluded, if it's been held for five years or more. This is subject to the exclusion limit, which is the greater of:

1. $10 million worth of tax benefit from a single company.

2. 10 times the original cost basis.

Even though these gains are excluded from income tax, 7% of the exclusion has to be added back to your AMT as a "preference item".

This holding period means you have to be an early employee. But, if you're tempted to hold for a long time to get this treatment, I offer this advice my first tax accountant gave me: "There is no tax manipulation you can do that outweighs the benefit of selling high."

Section 1202 exclusion conditions and calculations are so complex that if you think you qualify for them, you should consider hiring an accountant to make cross all the Is and dot all the Ts, or vice versa.

Example: *Alyssa P. Hacker joined ABC Corporation as its first employee, when its market cap was only $100,000. She exercised $10,000 worth of stock in 2005, and in 2011 ended up owning 10% of the now $500 million company. If she now sells $20 million worth of ABC Corporation, she can exclude $5 million of the sale's capital gains. The other $15 million will be taxed at regular long term capital gains tax rates. (Note that this is more* *than 10 times the original cost basis, which would be $100,000, because the higher exclusion limit applies) Unfortunately, when calculating AMT income, Alyssa can only exclude $4,650,000, since 7% of the exclusion is considered a "preference item".*

Moving out of state

In late 2003 and early 2004, Google opened an office in Kirkland, Washington. Streams of old-timers quickly moved there from California. The reason? Washington has no state income tax, while California's state income tax is 9.3% (10.3% for those making over $1 million a year). California doesn't provide a separate, lower tax rate for capital gains (short or long term). For a $10 million portfolio, that's $1 million in taxes just for living in California. Many employees with no California attachments chose to pack up and move instead of paying the tax.

I don't generally recommend such a move to other engineers. Moving away from Silicon Valley generally means losing access to its vibrant startup community. However, these employees had made a life-changing amount of money such that they never had to work at another job. In order to arrange such a move and have the tax consequences work out in your favor, you have to do the following:

1. Exercise all your stock options. Unexercised options earned in California and then sold are considered income earned in California and therefore subject to California state taxes.

2. Establish residency in another state (preferably one with no income taxes). How to do this varies from state to state. In Washington state, it was a matter of setting up a bank account, acquiring a Washington driver's license or identity card, and ensuring that all mail is addressed to a location in Washington.

3. Give up residency in California. This means selling your California house if you have one, closing bank accounts and other business interests in California (if you hold stock in other Silicon Valley startups, you'll want to consult a lawyer as to whether those stock holdings keep you a California resident). If you draw a salary or any income from any California property, this could

be difficult.

4. Not return to California for business purposes. You're still allowed to vacation there.

As you can see, doing all this is significant work (though #1 is almost always recommended anyway). In particular, if you ever wish to return to California at all, you'll end up paying back taxes unless you've taken care to document your intent to make the move permanent.

Example: A California executive, Jake Mobile, accepted an offer from a Californian company to run its Japanese subsidiary. Jake went to Japan for 11 years, running the business there and enjoying himself. Since he wasn't living in California, he didn't file California income taxes. His California home stayed empty.

After returning to California, he moved back into his house and started a new job at a different company (this time, one without any international subsidiaries). He then discovered that the Franchise Tax Board (FTB) claimed that he was a California resident all along, and hadn't intended to move away permanently. He therefore owed California 11 years of back taxes. He consulted with tax attorneys, but they told him that since he'd held on to his California home and moved back to it, he'd clearly intended to return to California all along. He was forced to pay the back taxes.

By far the biggest problem with making such moves for tax purposes is that unless you're positive the stock will stay at the same level (or higher), delaying stock sales for tax purposes can cost you far more than the tax savings from leaving California.

Sue Timing joined Google in October 2003. She wisely exercised all her stock options immediately upon receiving them. On November 7th, 2007, Google stock had reached $711 upon closing. Sue Timing still hadn't sold any of her stock, and decided to move to Nevada to establish residency. She quit her job, cut all ties with California, and moved to Nevada by Dec 30th 2007. By the time January 4th rolled around, however, Google stock had dropped from the high of $711 to $657. This drop in stock price had negated most of the advantage of moving to Nevada, and Sue unwisely decided to hang on to her stock. Unfortunately, the stock market was reacting to a financial crisis, and the stock kept dropping to a low of $262.43 on November 21st, 2008. Her attempt to game the tax system had cost her over $449/share, far negating any *advantage from moving out of state.*

Moving out of country

If you aren't a US citizen, and come from a country with low taxes or no capital gains tax, the ultimate tax dodge is to move out of the US entirely. You shouldn't make this move lightly. I'd only recommend this if you make a life-changing amount of money and wanted to move back home anyway.

Example: A friend of mine from Singapore moved back after five years at a startup and two years after its IPO. He cut all ties to the US after moving there, and used the international branch of an American brokerage. Since he was not a U.S. resident, and Singapore had no capital gains taxes, he paid $0 in capital gains on all stock sales.

Example: Switzerland's tax system is one where its various cantons (similar to states) compete for your taxes. If a Swiss citizen were to return after making a large sum of money in the USA, he could negotiate with all the cantons as to which he'd establish residency in.

The Swiss citizen also wouldn't owe any US taxes on stock sold as a resident and citizen in the country, owing only the amount negotiated with his now resident canton. A former Googler managed to negotiate a capital gains tax rate of 0% with the canton he moved to.

Note that this option is only available if you aren't a U.S. citizen. If you are, then you owe U.S. Federal taxes no matter where in the world you reside. You do get a tax break for the taxes paid to a non-U.S. country as a result of your residency, but the net effect on your taxes is that you end up paying either U.S. taxes or taxes in your country of residence, whichever is higher.

Also, if you try to dodge this tax by renouncing your citizenship, as of 2009 there's an "exit tax" when you do so. It effectively treats all your assets as being sold at market price the day you renounce your citizenship, and taxes you on that amount as income.

Since this kicks in at $600,000 in assets, the only way to dodge it would be to give up your citizenship before you had that much. And that would make continued Silicon Valley employment challenging to say the least.

Unlike California, if you're a non-US citizen, you can return to the US for business purposes after your departure. Three years after you leave, you can return to the US without being liable for any back taxes on the stocks you sold. Note that if you return to California, you could still be liable for back taxes there!

Charitable remainder trusts

Irrevocable charitable remainder trusts work as follows:

1. The donor commit assets to the trust. It has two sets of beneficiaries: income beneficiaries, and remainder beneficiaries which must be charities. The trust is **irrevocable**. What this means is that any money you commit to the trust cannot be moved out of the trust, other than the income the trust generates for the income beneficiaries.

2. The assets donated to the trust are exempt from taxes and are no longer considered part of the donor's estate. All profit from investment sales within the trust are not subject to taxes.

3. The trustee manages the assets in the trust. The trustee can be the same person as the donor.

4. The beneficiaries draw a set amount of income annually paid from the trust. This must be at least 5% of the assets in the trust. However, the trust income is subject to income taxes.

5. When the donor passes away, the trust's remainder beneficiaries then own all its assets.

The **irrevocable** part of the trust should give you pause. This isn't money that goes to your heirs, or for any purpose other than charity. If you need more than the fixed withdrawal amount you set, then you'll have to get it from other sources.

If you do set up a charitable remainder trust, I recommend that doing so only after discussion with a lawyer and an accountant. Even then, only commit money to it you would've donated to a charity anyway.

During the middle part of the last decade, many university endowments did extremely well. At that point, many wealthy folks were tempted to set up charitable remainder trusts with one as the remainder beneficiary in order to have the trust monies managed by the high performing endowment. However, such endowments aren't all run equally well, so I'd be very wary of doing this.

Final words about taxes

When I met with my first tax accountant and got him to explain to me what AMT was he said "No amount of tax planning can overcome the disadvantage of not selling high. Conversely, if you sell high, you don't have to do as much tax planning to successfully reach your goals."

Having written more about tax planning in this chapter than I intended to, I want to make one thing clear. Ethically, we owe taxes to the society that creates an environment that makes our work possible. To the extent that society values our work and rewards us, the taxes that we pay also go into supporting and maintaining that society. I don't consider tax an evil in and of itself. While doing tax planning is useful and important, I wouldn't advocate using any questionable or illegal schemes to hide your income from the government, or using the tax shelters frequently sold by accounting firms or investment banks to dodge taxes. In general, plans that haven't had an explicit IRS ruling are ethically and legally questionable. Tax evasion penalties are serious, and can cost you much more than the taxes saved.

Paying taxes isn't a bad thing—if nothing else, it means you've made money. In particular, there are very few places with the same energetic people, beautiful climate, plentiful jobs, and natural beauty as Silicon Valley, and I consider the benefits more than justify the taxes paid to the state of California. If you're tempted to dodge taxes, ask yourself this question; is there anywhere else other than Silicon Valley where you could've received the support necessary to make the large sums of money while doing work you enjoy?

Summary

Exercise your stock options if you work at a privately held company and believe the company will become more valuable. Conversely, if you no longer believe that the startup will be valuable, what are you doing there?

File an 83b election if you exercise your options to ensure long term capital gains treatment of any stock you sell.

No amount of tax planning will save you if you don't sell high.

Further reading

Consider your options: Get the most from your equity compensation. Kaye A. Thomas. Fairmark Press (revised annually) (http://goo.gl/8MMO)

Taxvisor. http://www.taxvisor.com. Geoff Mendal, updated annually. Your best source for predicting what AMT will do to you. (http://goo.gl/s4Xz)

Perfectly Legal: The Covert Campaign to Rig Our Tax System to Benefit the Super Rich—and Cheat Everybody Else. David Cay Johnston, Portfolio Trade, 2005. Case study after case study of tax cheats (some of whom got caught, and many who didn't). Don't read this book in the months leading up to April 15th. (http://goo.gl/KoA4)

6

Leaving Your Startup

All good things must come to an end, even work you enjoy. If you've done everything you wanted to do at a startup, it may be time to leave. This chapter covers the reasons to leave, and how to do so gracefully.

Why should you leave?

Many engineers tend to stay at a failing startup for too long, wasting the opportunity to seek out a company with a better chance of success. But that's not the only reason to leave:

- You've stayed at the company long enough to vest all of your initial grant of stock options, and the corporation hasn't granted you refresher options. This is a sign that your services aren't appreciated, and you should start an aggressive search. If you've been getting regular promotions, they should've also come with additional stock grants. Some startups don't automatically provide stock grants with a promotion. If that's true (and it should be pretty apparent if you ask the management team), you should negotiate for it when you get your promotion.

- A better opportunity comes up, and you like it so much that you're willing to give up whatever's left of your existing stock compensation to take it. This is by far the best reason to leave—in particular, getting a promotion and substantial (15% or more) raise for a new job should signal that you're currently undervalued. You should either immediately start negotiating for a raise, or leave for a new job as quickly as possible. Every day you work at your current job costs you 15% of your salary!

- You've a burning desire to start your own company. Congratulations! Most people never take this step. If you've got a great idea and can execute it, there's no reason to wait. Remember that your employment contract probably specifies that all your inventions as an employee belong to your current company. So before you start executing your idea, you need to resign. Otherwise, you may discover that all your hard work belongs to someone else.

- You don't see an opportunity for success at the company. This can either be because your career's stalled out, or because the company isn't going anywhere. In particular, it's a red flag if the company has launched several dud products but isn't changing direction. You'll just waste any more time you spend there.

- **No external funding.** After building the initial prototype and getting users for the product, the founders' next step is to raise money to fund the startup. Very wealthy founders may fund the startup themselves. If so, watch how the funding happens; it should be treated like a regular Angel round, and the founders should put in money all at once. Dribbling money into the company a bit every month can result in substantial dilution of employee holdings. In particular, if the founders were wealthy enough to fund their own startup, but couldn't find venture capitalists willing to invest, it could be a signal that they've burned their VC bridges—not a good sign.

- **No external board members.** Board members act as a sanity check for executives, and can force a CEO change in extreme cases. By keeping all board seats in the hands of people close to the founders, there might be no checks on whatever the executives want to do, including turning down lucrative acquisitions.

- **Founders being forced out.** It takes a lot for a founder to abandon a company he started. If the founders are leaving, it's time for you to leave. What's left is often a shell of a company.

- **Acquisitions made without an adequate business case.** For instance, there was no reason for Excite and @Home to have merged. It showed that venture capitalists were trying to manage their portfolios by merging the companies, rather than the officers and directors trying to do what was best for the shareholders and employees.

- **Founders/Board turns down a lucrative sale**. Obviously there are many exceptions to this rule: both Facebook and Google turned down $1B offers and went on to be much bigger successes. However, unless the business is sustainably profitable, turning down such big offers is foolhardy. One of the startups I worked for turned down a $750M acquisition offer despite being unprofitable. If I'd been integrated deeply enough into the grapevine to have heard about it, I would've started looking for a job right away. The company was later shuttered and all my stock became worthless.

- **Revolving door for executives.** Engineering organizations require stability at the top level. If the company goes through multiple vice-presidents of engineering within 18 months, that's a red flag that it can't attract suitable engineering management.

- **Top engineers departing for competitors or other ventures**. This is a biggie, especially if these engineers are also early employees. Management will always try to put a good spin on it, but if a company is doing well and is pleasant to work for, there's very little incentive for early employees and top engineers to leave.

- **Company focused more on lawsuits than on products**. If the products and sales are successful, lawsuits are a distraction. Conversely, if those aren't working out, there's a strong incentive to sue your way into profitability. In either case, there's very little room for engineers to play a role in the company.

When should you leave?

As previously mentioned, you should stay at least long enough to initially vest. That's a minimum of a year at most startups. Since the range of outcomes is rarely predictable at startups, even if you think the business won't succeed, you might be wrong. It could easily take a year to build enough of the product to tell one way or another.

Beyond that, there are a few other factors to consider:

Leaving Your Startup

- If you don't already have another job lined up, it's a good idea to start your job search and check the market before leaving. Not only does it make your negotiation easier, it might also provide a comparison with your current startup. It could be that after a few conversations with other startups, you'd reconsider your decision.

- Try to time your departure for right after a vesting event (i.e. a monthly anniversary of your start date, or your initial vesting cliff, rather than a week earlier) if you're still vesting substantial amount of stock. It might sound like micro-optimization, but since you have control over when you leave, why not do so?

What to do before you leave

Exercise all your eligible stock options. Typical stock options expire 90 days after you leave the company, though some may expire in as little as 30 or 60 days. Make sure you check the stock option contract to see how much time you have. If you've pre-exercised all your options, then you don't have to do anything—the onus is on the company to buy back any unvested options.

Say goodbye to everyone in a courteous manner. Now isn't the time to burn any bridges—remember, it's a very small valley, and anyone you've met could easily end up determining if you get hired at the next hot startup. If you can, leave your personal e-mail address with friends and colleagues so that they can still contact you.

Please note that non-compete (and non-solicit) agreements are in force, so you can't recruit other employees. However, you should consider making a list of undervalued engineers who'd make prime recruits for when your non-solicit agreement expires.

When you interview while considering leaving your current company, it's frequently tempting to tell interviewers everything you consider responsible for your employer's upcoming failure. It's very important that you resist this temptation with all your strength.

Bad-mouthing your current employer reflects badly on you, and I strongly recommend that you stick to what your mother told you, "If you can't say anything nice, don't say anything at all".

What to do after you leave

If you don't already have another job lined up or aren't starting work right away, it's a good idea to have the COBRA continued health insurance paperwork handy and signed. Note that small companies of less than 20 people are exempt from COBRA, so if you're working at such a company, find out if it's available.

You have 60 days to enroll after you leave, and it's up to you to meet all the deadlines for applying and paying premiums. If you take a vacation, for, say, four weeks, between the two jobs or have an accident and can't start your new job, you need to get the paperwork in to keep having health insurance. For peace of mind, I recommend either signing up right away and paying the premiums, or leaving the signed paperwork with a trusted person who can file it for you if you're incapacitated.

If the startup folds

If you've exercised your options and the startup folds, is liquidated, or sold at a price lower than the options you paid, you can claim a capital loss on the exercised options. The difference between the price you paid and the amount you received for your shares can then be deducted against capital gains, or up to $3000 against your income that year. Any additional losses can be carried over indefinitely and used to offset income at the rate of $3000 a year or any future capital gains, until the total amount you've offset equals your loss.

Surviving an acquisition or rapid growth

An acquisition by another big company or rapid growth into big companies are disruptive changes that will make your startup into a much different place to work. While some people adapt naturally into a larger organization, many cannot or choose not to, indicating that large corporations are not suited for them.

Ex-Googler Fritz Schneider[1] left Google to join startup Aardvark, which was then acquired by Google in 2010. He has the following tips for start-

---

1   E-mail sent to private ex-Googler mailing list. Quoted with permission.

up engineers who choose to stay on after an acquisition by a large corporation or rapid growth:

- Align yourself with someone of influence who you respect, and who prizes his or her reports. I realized I was irrelevant in one Product Area and went looking for someone at the VP, Director, or Principal level to whom I could make myself useful if not indispensable. I found that person and started taking on unsexy tasks that were a burden to him. I set up a relationship where I was taking problems off his plate so he didn't have to worry about them. I refer to this as taking bricks out of his backpack. Good people who prize their reports will appreciate that, and think of you for the next big opportunity.

- Align yourself with what's important to {the company, Product Area, VP, your manager; the higher the level the better}. Almost everything that a big company like Google does comes top-down; it's nearly impossible for something to happen bottom up at this point. So I spend time listening to OKR meetings, TGIFs, all hands, and so forth, and try to find opportunities that are aligned.

- Forge relationships across the org. Either working with teams in other product areas or switching areas. You have to spend sufficient time in one place to have a big impact, but once you have a few wins, it really pays dividends to branch out. So many people are siloed at Google these days that those of us who aren't can really make a big difference.

- Apply leverage. Nothing important at Google can be done by one or two people. You need leverage, meaning people helping you pull in the direction you're heading. This likely means less individual contributor activities and more managing and leading, or if you prefer, polishing your powers of persuasion and getting others to do what you want them to. Taking reports is a good start. Find someone else to spend time on the mundane stuff so you can concentrate on delivering strategic value.

- Don't try to trade on old accomplishments. No one cares, and many even resent that you still feel entitled for something awesome you did four years ago. You have to continue to stack up successes. There's real, significant resentment for the I'm-an-oldtimer-so-I'm-going-to-do-what-I-want attitude. It's just not useful.

Now I'm not saying I'm particularly relevant at this point. I'm actually not so much. But I'm much more so that I would've been without realizing that Google has changed, and that I needed to change how I worked in response. You really can still do things that impact billions of people, but to a large extent doing so requires humbling yourself and getting with the program dictated by Larry et al. Not everyone will be happy with that—I certainly have limited appetite for it—but from my perspective that's the way big companies work. If it sounds more like a job than a passion, well, maybe it is.

Further reading

Career Warfare. David F D'Alessandro with Michele Owens. McGraw Hill, 2004. An insightful look at how big company politics work, including many tips on how to get ahead in that environment. (http://goo.gl/2CY40)

7

Basic Financial Planning for Engineers

It's beyond this book's scope to provide a comprehensive financial planning guide. However, when I've advised some medium to high net worth folk, I've seen them make financial planning mistakes. I can at least tell you what to not to do.

The basics

It never fails to surprise me that even these basic common sense financial things seem to be hard for people to do:

- Avoid credit card debt.

- Make full use of tax-deferred savings accounts.

- Never pay retail prices for big items.

- Make a will or put together a living trust for your assets.

- Treat housing as a consumption expense, not a highly leveraged investment instrument.

- Avoid get rich quick schemes.

- Do most your investing in low-expense passive securities that are adequately diversified.

Mindset changes

When advising other engineers, it usually isn't the required intelligence or ability to understand sound investing that're their problems, but rather their mindset. It always astounds me how much someone's identity is tied up with what he does and who he thinks he is, rather than who he wants to be and what he actually wants to achieve.

When I first joined Google, I spent about an hour explaining to a new engineer the advantages of early exercise. At any other company, it might've been a risky move, but Google was still publishing a daily revenue figure chart on an internal home page that all employees had access to. So we knew the company was doing well.

I calculated that pre-exercising would save approximately 25% of his eventual stock option worth in taxes, but he came up with one excuse after another. "I don't have cash to early exercise with." "Ask your your dad if you could borrow money from him and pay him back with interest." "No, that would give him a heart attack. He'd think that I'd become a responsible adult." "OK, I'll loan you the money, you'd just have to split the tax savings with me." "No, that's too sophisticated for me." The total cost of maintaining his self-image was probably about $500,000.

Another person didn't set up a 401(k) plan even though the company matched 50% of whatever she put into it. This was an incredibly generous match, but for her, setting up an investment account would also mean becoming an adult. Not doing so meant giving up $7,500 a year in free money, if she'd contributed the maximum amount.

It's very important to let go of the perception that you're still a child if you want to be a successful investor or hold on to any money you make. When you wake up in the morning, just look at yourself in the mirror and say, "I am an adult. I choose whether to go to school or work. I choose to be responsible for myself and my assets and those whom I hold dear." Say that enough times and you'll find yourself able to act contrary to your previous self-image.

Avoid credit card debt

Credit card debt carries an incredibly high interest rate, frequently in excess of 15%. If you tried to get an investment return of 15% or more, you'd discover that you'd have make incredibly risky investments. So instead of you giving such high returns to financial institutions, avoid such debt in the first place.

I don't shun credit cards—many provide valuable rewards. If you pay off such cards every month, you don't pay the usurious interest and get an effective 1-2% discount on your purchases. Just avoid paying annual fees, which can easily eat up any gains from the rewards.

Make full use of tax-deferred accounts

Most startups don't match your 401(k) contributions. While a 401(k)'s tax-deferment is extremely valuable, there's no real advantage if the fund selection is so poor that a self-managed IRA can outperform it, even though you can't put as much money into it.

A good 401(k) plan has a selection of low-cost indexed funds (typically from Fidelity or Vanguard), but many small company 401(k) plans are run by administrators who get kickbacks from a mutual fund company. Those kickbacks are paid for by the fund charging a front-end load, a back-end load, or outrageously high fees.

IRAs behave the same as 401(k)s as far as tax deferment is concerned, but only if you meet certain requirements. Since most engineers get a decent salary, the only way to get a tax-deferred IRA is not to enroll in your employer's 401(k).

To set up a tax-deferred IRA, ask any mutual fund company (I recommend Vanguard—http://www.vanguard.com) to open one for you. You can then buy any fund you like. The caveat here is to keep your tax-deferred IRAs, rollover IRAs, and post-tax IRAs separate. I don't recommend post-tax IRAs, because they complicate accounting when you finally start taking money out of your IRAs.

The difference between an IRA and a 401(k) is that 401(k)s shelter up to

$15,000 of income per year, while an IRA can only shelter $4,000 a year.

Income versus capital gains

The tax code give a favorable rate for long term capital gains in order to encourage investment. To qualify for long term capital gains, you must hold the investment for more than a year. While short term capital gains and income are taxed at ordinary income tax rates (which can be more than 45% for state and federal taxes if you live in California), federal long term capital gains rates are currently at an all time low of 15% (or 25% if you also pay California taxes).

Whenever you can, you should try to qualify for long term capital gains. Early exercising your stock options is a good move because it turns what would otherwise be income (if your startup is successful) into capital gains.

I once compared my total lifetime income with a friend who became a professor at a major university. In terms of total income, we were paid about the same. While a professor's salary was somewhat lower, he more than made up for that by also doing consulting work. The difference between our net worths was entirely due to my turning what otherwise would've been classified as regular income into capital gains.

In addition, capital losses from losing money in an investment can be deducted from capital gains to reduce taxable income. If your capital losses exceed your capital gains in a given year, you can deduct up to $3000 against your regular income for that year, **and** carry what's left over to the next year, when you get to repeat the process. You can do this every year until the loss has been completely applied to either capital gains or regular income.

This is called tax loss harvesting. In order to tax-loss harvest, you must sell your investment at a loss, and wait at least 30 days before buying the same security again. If you do buy it back within 30 days, it's considered a wash sale, and you don't get to record a capital loss.

Asset allocation in your 401(k) accounts

Entire books have been written about asset allocation. If you're at all interested in financial planning, I strongly recommend you read one.

However, if you're not interested in financial planning, then I recommend you use one of the many available "one-stop" life-cycle funds. Vanguard calls them the "Target-Retirement" fund series, where each fund's matched to a target retirement date. The date determines how aggressively each fund is invested.

A younger investor has a longer time horizon and can afford to allocate more of his portfolio in stocks. But an investor nearing retirement wouldn't want to jeopardize his retirement by being so invested in stocks in case of a sudden stock market collapse.

Never pay retail for large items

The really big items you buy and sell are cars and houses. In both cases, the items are so profitable that dedicated sales people sell them to you one-on-one. Both are frequently financed, allowing sales people to apply such tricks as "How much of a monthly payment can you afford?"

By approaching typical consumers in this way, sales people frequently fool them into buying much more house or car than they need, and spending beyond their means.

Houses aren't fungible commodities (you can't treat all houses the same way). But cars are, so you want to get car dealers bidding against each other. Once you've decided which car model you want by test driving and reading reviews, send e-mail to or fax every dealer of that car within a 200 mile radius and ask for quotes. Specify the desired car as much as you can, including trim level, important options, and undesirable colors.

Take the three lowest bids, call up the dealers, and get them to bid against each other. Then take the lowest deal. You can even, as a last measure, take the lowest bid to your nearest dealer and ask if they'll match it, so you don't have to drive as far to pick up the car.

I've always bought new cars this way and been satisfied. Unfortunately, you can't buy used cars this way since they aren't fungible commodities.

Make a will or set up a living trust

If you don't own substantial property, or most of your property is in the form of financial assets (bank accounts or mutual fund accounts), you can skip this if you fill out the beneficiary statement with your accounts' firms. These accounts bypass probate and the other inheritance issues, making a will or living trust unnecessary for them.

However, once you have a house, car, or any other titled asset, you must plan to skip probate after your death. You don't want your house tied up in probate. Silicon Valley houses are so expensive that, while in probate, your estate will be stuck with substantial property taxes. If the house can't be lived in or rented out during probate, your estate will lose substantial income.

There are several ways to do this, the easiest being owning the property with your desired beneficiary as joint owners with right of survivorship. This means when one of you dies, the other person owns the property free and clear. The downsides are that everything has to be owned jointly, and, if you change your mind later, you can't change the beneficiary without your joint owner's consent.

A less permanent solution is a living trust. You set up a trust that owns all your property with yourself as the trust's controller. You designate a new trustee to take over in the event of your death, which dissolves the trust. This avoids probate but not estate taxes. Most people hire a lawyer to setup a living trust. This can be useful if you're the kind of person who would set up a living trust but then forget to re-title your property so that the trust owns it instead of you. If you are capable of remembering to do so, setting up a trust is mostly a matter of copying and pasting boilerplate language and you can do it without a lawyer by reading the Nolo Press book: **Make Your Own Living Trust**.

If you have no dependents or other family that you care about, then you probably don't care about probate and can just rely on the beneficiary statements of your financial institutions.

Treat housing as a consumption expense

The conventional wisdom regarding housing is to mortgage yourself to the hilt and buy as expensive a house as you can. The reasoning is that while your income grows over time, inflation erodes away your debt's value. But startup employees can hardly count on gradually increasing income, and the housing crisis of 2008-2010 has shown that depending on house prices to always go up is a mistake.

Housing is special because it's usually purchased as a highly leveraged product. This multiplies your upside if it happens, but also multiplies your downside if prices drop. Given the many times a typical American moves, and the large buying and selling transaction costs involved, your best housing move is to do what Warren Buffett did. Namely, buy a house you'll live in for 30 years or so.

Historically, the Case-Shiller index for house prices has gone up about 1% a year nationwide over the last 50 years. This is a far cry from the 3% real return the equity investments have seen over a similar period.

This means if you have spare cash, you're likely better off over the long term by buying more equity than by buying a bigger house. Ownership of a larger house also means you'll pay more in both property taxes and maintenance costs.

Avoid get rich quick schemes

In particular, many people fall prey to "alternative-income" stories, whether working as a real estate agent or opening a chain restaurant. While holding a full time startup job, it's more important to work on your strengths and avoid your weaknesses than to try to develop another line of business.

Asian engineers seem to fall prey to this more frequently than non-Asians, mostly because they come from countries where most real wealth is built on real estate. Because of this, Asian parents seem to be more pushy about getting their children to buy a house early, or to buy too much house.

In general, I like to tell people that if you're an engineer because you enjoy engineering, why not do more of it, rather than trying to start a different career? If you don't enjoy engineering, startups probably aren't interesting to you anyway, since a large company 9-to-5 job provides more stability and more time to pursue other interests and career options.

A good startup is probably the best legal *get rich quick* scheme out there, and, in my opinion, you're always better off investing more time into either the startup or leisure time that lets you recover from a startup's frequently intense pressure, rather than trying an alternative business.

Jeff Rothschild (VP of Technology at Facebook) once said to me, "What's the best way to make a small fortune as an angel investor? Start with a large one." If you've succeeded at a startup, it's frequently advantageous to fund new startups. I'd encourage you to do this, but only with a very small, less than 5%, portion of your portfolio.

Startups do have a relatively high failure rate. Unless you have a strong belief in the startup's technology and a significant ability to affect a start-up's outcome, you have to invest in a fairly large number of startups to mitigate the risks of their individual failures.

Most people don't have a large enough portfolio such that tying up $50,000 of capital per startup for up to 10 years wouldn't hurt if about 75% of them failed by the 5 year mark. Whenever I've invested in start-ups, I consider the money immediately lost, and don't consider it when evaluating my current net worth.

I will note that of the people I know personally who made themselves wealthy, the ones who've suffered massive loss of wealth have not lost their money through profligarate spending, but rather by investing in get rich quick schemes without thought.

Have a portfolio of passive investments

I consider this advice appropriate for people in startups because of the following:

- It's passive—once you've set up a portfolio, you don't have to do much. At most, you have to rebalance it once a year, something easily accomplished in a couple of hours with a spreadsheet.

- You can customize it according to how much risk you want to take.

- There is an abundance of literature about the topic, and you can buy one-stop solutions (as previously mentioned), or dive in and break down your asset allocation into micro-segments if you enjoy that sort of thing. Doing so doesn't automatically mean you get better results—John Greaney has a web page where he notes that a simple S&P 500/Treasury portfolio has, over the last 10 years or so, beaten the complex portfolios designed by asset allocation guru William Bernstein!

- It's cheap! Expense ratios below 0.2% per year are possible with passive investments. That means less money to the financial "engineers" on Wall Street and more money for you.

How much is enough?

If you ask a collection of people how much money they'd want to have in order to retire, you'll get a wide range of answers. The reason is that most people really have no idea how much money it'd take to safely generate a steady annual income stream over several decades.

According to the safe withdrawal studies at the Retire Early Home Page, over a 60 year period a diversified portfolio can throw off about 3% worth of spending money a year and not run out. Shorter time frames mean that the safe withdrawal rate can be higher. But since you can't tell if the worst has already happened, a real life result of around 2% might provide a bigger margin of safety. This means that if you need an inflation-adjusted income stream of $100,000 a year, you'll want a portfolio of at least a bit over $3 million.

This illustrates why financial planners focus so much on living below your means. Each dollar of yearly spending money requires an additional $33 in your portfolio. Furthermore, since that dollar of spending comes from after tax money, you really need to generate closer to $1.3 of spending money for every dollar you actually spend (more if you live in a state with high income taxes).

In his book Succeeding, John T. Reed describes how setting his financial goals too high caused him to take unnecessary risk, resulting in a smaller net worth when some risks didn't pay off. Setting financial goals too high can actually be harmful to your financial health!

Hiring a financial planner

A lot of financial planning books recommend hiring a financial planner to handle your investments rather than doing it yourself. The thought seems to be that most people don't have the time or the inclination to study up on such a complex subject as financial planning and hence should outsource the work to a paid professional. Paul Buchheit, in a May 2010 blog post[1] providing tips for new millionaires, points out that you should not hire a financial advisor without first learning about how to manage your money. Unfortunately, most people, software engineers included, who hire financial advisors know less about how to interview one than a marketing person would know about how to interview a software engineer.

However, if you are a competent software engineer, you probably have the intellectual capacity to do your own financial planning—coding in C++ or Javascript is far tougher than creating asset-allocation spreadsheets. Where things fall apart is having sufficient emotional control as to not sell into a crisis and not get greedy and buy just because the market's doing well. The discipline behind buy-low and sell-high in a passive portfolio is called **rebalancing**. The idea here is that whenever you deviate from your original asset allocation, you would sell the over-performing assets to buy the under-performing assets to return to your target asset allocation. Doing so ensures that when there's irrational exuberance in one asset, you will be selling that asset in order to buy other assets.

My experience is that most engineers that get into trouble with doing their own financial planning fail to rebalance because they try to outsmart the rebalancing system. The solution then is to either hire an agent to do this rebalancing or to automate the system. A human agent who is emotionally detached from your portfolio should theoretically be able to rebalance your portfolio correctly. However, humans are expensive and also subject to conflicts of interest—as Scott Burns wrote, "Rented brains feel a deep spiritual need to build 20,000-square-foot log cabins in Jackson Hole with the return on our money."

I've interviewed financial planners, both for myself and for clients. My impression at this point is that most of the successful ones are pretty much glorified salespeople: most of them are incapable of answering

---

1   http://paulbuchheit.blogspot.com/2010/05/what-to-do-with-your-millions.html

questions such as, "If I had a balanced portfolio worth $N million, what is the maximum safe withdrawal rate that will ensure that I won't run out of money in 60 years?" They will hem and haw and then provide an answer that's either too conservative (forgone consumption during your life time), or overly aggressive (causing you to deplete your portfolio too early).

As far as automation is concerned, one Silicon Valley startup has written the necessary automation. Wealthfront provides a financial planning/ asset manager service for individuals. After interviewing you about your financial preferences and tolerance for risk, the company's software automatically sets up a portfolio with a customized (for your risk tolerance, age, and financial circumstances) asset allocation, and then periodically rebalances your portfolio for you. The cost for this service is 0.25% of your assets per year (with the first $25,000 of the portfolio free of charges). This is cheapest than all but the most conscientious fee-based financial advisors, and if you're not capable of sticking rigorously to an asset allocation, they would be a good bet.[2]

If you do strike it rich

If your startup does have a liquidity event resulting in your having a high net worth, I strongly encourage you to read **all** the books listed below. The time you spend doing so will likely be the most highly compensated hours in your life.

Furthermore, if you do hit this proverbial jackpot, keep in mind that highly concentrated stock portfolios are very risky. It's a good idea to diversify your portfolio even if you take an immediate hit on taxes or on potential future capital gains. A lot of Silicon Valley veterans had to learn this lesson the hard way during the dot.com crash of 2001-2002 and the financial crisis of 2007-2008. You're strongly urged to learn from their mistakes.

The biggest financial mistakes people make is in trying to maximize their portfolio, rather than ensuring that their nest egg is safe. Your worst enemy is your own greed.

---

2   I am neither a customer of nor investor in Wealthfront (http://vip.wealthfront.com).

Further reading

The Dilbert guide to personal finance. Scott Adams. This is the best starting point for financial planning. It takes 5 minutes to read. (http://goo.gl/vj0G)

A Random Walk Down Wall Street. Burton S. Malkiel, W. W. Norton & Company, 2007 (revised frequently). The classic book on stock markets and still one of the best books on the topic. (http://goo.gl/GcU3)

The Intelligent Asset Allocator. William Bernstein, McGraw Hill, 2000. A highly technical treatise on asset allocation, but it dvocates a complex portfolio that might not return better results than a simpler portfolio. (http://goo.gl/bY0o) If you find this book is too technical, try Bernstein's **An Investor's Manifesto** (McGrawHill 2009). (http://goo.gl/4NkI)

Unconventional Success: A Fundamental Approach to Personal Investment. David F. Swensen, Free Press, 2005. This book covers advanced topics, but is chiefly useful in its description of which mutual fund companies deserve your trust. There are so few trustworthy companies that he provides the names of all three. (http://goo.gl/H8Cs)

The Retire Early Home Page, John Greaney. This is the classic web page on retiring early and safe-withdrawal rate studies. It contains many spreadsheets for planning purposes, as well as real life case studies. There's also a comprehensive discussion on the SEPP 72(t) exception, which is useful for early retirees. It's updated frequently and its forums are a wealth of expertise on various approaches to retirement. The early retirement personality study, for instance, indicates that engineers are more likely to fare well in retirement than any other profession. (http://goo.gl/fRC0)

Succeeding. John T. Reed, John T. Reed Publishing, 2009. This is a great book in general, and has an entire chapter devoted to summarizing the above investing books. It has a section that the other books don't cover, which is "what's an appropriate financial goal". (http://goo.gl/FkbY)

Make Your Own Living Trust. Denis Clifford, Nolo Press 2009. A great book explaining living trusts and how they work. You don't even need a lawyer. If you're not sure you need a living trust, Clifford's **Plan Your Estate** is a good starting point. (http://goo.gl/6jE2)

What To Do With Your Millions. Paul Buchheit, Blog Post 2010. A great blog post for new millionaires. (http://goo.gl/zaQBN)

John T. Reed's Sensible Shopping List For The Rich. John T. Reed, undated web page. A practical and unexciting shopping list. (http://goo.gl/dBKEZ)

8

My Startup Story

I've spent the better part of a 17 year Silicon Valley career at startups. In this chapter, I'll go over my history and detail lessons I learned along the way, which will hopefully illustrate the previous chapters' contents.

Geoworks

I worked for Geoworks in 1991 as a software engineering intern. The previous year, I'd felt under-challenged at an internship at Bellcore. Jimmy Lefkowitz and Larry Hosken, then Geoworks interns, recruited me and the interview process was both challenging and fun. Geoworks set aside an "intern candidate interview" day, during which candidates were shuttled from one interview room to another. Each room had a pair of full time engineers who'd pose problems and ask us to solve them on the whiteboards.

Geoworks was building a new operating system for IBM PC-compatible machines, one with a GUI, built-in pre-emptive multitasking, and with enough interesting applications to be useful out of the box. This happened during the heady days of shrink-wrapped software and everything seemed possible, even beating Microsoft at the GUI-based operating system game.

Geoworks built everything in assembly language. The kernel had to fit within an 8086 segment, or 64KB, which meant every time something was added to it, bytes had to be saved elsewhere. Most of the development was done on Sun workstations attached to PCs. The application or operating system was downloaded to the PC, and then executed or debugged through a smart debugger.

Geoworks devoted a huge amount of energy into building tools (this is characteristic of successful technology companies). The assembler was written in-house, and in 1991 they already had a parallelized compilation and linking system. This enabled any engineer to use everyone's workstations to speed up his edit/compile/debug cycle. They also built their own GUI description language based mainly on Tcl/Tk, making dialog boxes and other GUI elements resolution independent.

Like many other technology startups, there was a dearth of management. There were maybe three engineering directors, and they spent more time writing code than managing. Engineers had leeway to work on "anarchy" projects, basically things they were passionate about but weren't seen as a high enough priority to be official assignments.

The freedom to work on projects of your choice is common for most startups. Google was only unusual in that it became a policy known as 20% time.

Larry Hosken had this to say about 20% at Geoworks:

> After your time, there was a little push for 20% at Geoworks. There was some new guy on the board and he suggested it. Managers excitedly walked up to engineers and said that we could spend 20% of our time on something we felt strongly about. Does that mean we'll push out the schedule on my current project? Uh, no, of course not. And that was the end of that.

Since there was well over 10 million lines of assembly code (even the applications were written in assembly), searching the codebase was a problem. There was a ctags-based tool, and engineers would use `vi -t` to jump to a function definition. But the time of running `vi -t` on such a large code base in 1991 was measured in minutes.

As a new engineer who had to learn a ton of this codebase to write my project (an e-mail application written entirely in assembly), I had an insight. If the entire codebase index was held in memory, the search response time could be reduced to sub-seconds. It was important to get to sub-second response time—otherwise the execution time interrupted engineers' programming flow. One weekend, I coded up the tool, including an Emacs editor extension that talked to the server.

The result of coding this tool was amazing. Overnight, even diehard vi users switched to Emacs just to get the benefit of the improved latency. Years later, I'd still be introduced to Geoworks engineers as the writer of the tags-server. I also later rewrote this tool at Google, where it was called gtags.

I left Geoworks after the summer for a pretty silly reason. They had the policy that part-timers were paid less than full-timers per hour, even interns, despite already getting less pay due to fewer hours. I quickly calculated that if I signed up to be an undergraduate teaching assistant for the undergrad compiler class I'd get the same pay, but not have to leave campus, so I signed up.

From what my friends at Geoworks told me, soon after I left all the former interns who were now part-time workers got a raise. The rest of my senior year, Geoworks kept trying to recruit me as a full time engineer, but my experience had me believing I wouldn't be adequately compensated if I joined.

While compensation isn't the be-all and end-all of employment, inadequate compensation is a good reason to look for a new job.

My intention was to go to graduate school and then into academia, so I applied to graduate schools and was admitted to three of my top choices (MIT, University of Washington, and UC Berkeley). However, what happened the summer after I graduated would change the course of my life.

Pure Software

At Bellcore, Sudhanshu "Suds" Jain asked me for some help with data structures. I spent an hour in his office explaining skip lists, hash tables, and other data structures. During that hour he somehow decided that I had potential.

After I finished my Bellcore internship, he left Bellcore to work in Silicon Valley at Adaptive Technologies, a chip startup. When he heard in 1992 that I was about to graduate, he mentioned to an Adaptive contractor that the contractor might want to consider hiring me.

That contractor was Reed Hastings, who was working at night and weekends in his basement on Purify. Suds connected us and I agreed to meet Reed at Pure Software's booth at the Software Development conference.

I arrived at the conference, but Reed had neglected to send a badge for me to reception, so I cajoled and talked my way in and showed up at the booth with a badge saying I was already an employee. When I walked up to Reed and introduced myself, he said "So, how much would you like to get paid for the summer?"

I told him Microsoft's offer, and he beat it by $300/month. I accepted the offer on the spot. At the time, I was amazed he didn't even bother giving me a technical interview (which Microsoft did in spades), but on reflection, I probably looked like a really low risk hire. If things didn't work out, I'd be gone by the summer anyway, and, as an intern, I was really cheap.

Over the summer, I worked on Quantify, Pure's followup product to Purify. It used the same technology as Purify to instrument code and get precise instruction-cycle level performance metrics.

However, what was more educational was getting a good look at how quickly a bootstrapped startup could reach profitability. Pure was incorporated in February 1992, and by April it was profitable. When Reed decided to get venture funding, he didn't need the money but felt he could use more help managing and growing the company.

By the end of the summer, Reed decided that he liked my work so much that he'd pay to keep me out of graduate school. He offered me 20% more than the going rate for a fresh graduate, and said "We'll kick you out of here in a year so you can go to graduate school." He further sweetened the pot with 3,000 shares at 3 cents a share, to be vested over one year. While I'd managed to get out of school with relatively little debt, this was such a large sum of money that I felt that I couldn't refuse.

That year, I learned a lot about startup software development. We all had the autonomy to do the work we needed to do. And when was time to hire a manager for Quantify, I helped interview candidates. Reed took special care to persuade me it was a sound hire.

Whenever there was a crisis (one involved Purify 2.0's garbage collector), everyone pitched in, including Reed. Even though he told everyone that Neil Hunt was a much better engineer, Reed was an excellent engineer. Reed's humility made an impression on everyone in the organization, myself included.

It was also quite clear that Pure Software had high standards. When an early engineer made several consecutive mistakes that broke the nightly builds, he was fired right away. I recruited several of my friends from Berkeley to work at Pure Software; Doug Orleans, Peng-Toh Sim, and Joe Chung. I also tried to get Steven Yen to join, but he turned us down to join Approach Software. I received Pure's first referral bonus.

At the end of the year, I had written all of Quantify's UI (which resulted in my disliking UI coding for the rest of my career), gotten my name on a patent, and generally had a great time. When it came time for me to leave for graduate school, I felt a lump in my throat.

However, before I left, I looked at my stock options contract and realized that I only had 60 days after leaving Pure to exercise my stock options. I therefore exercised all of them.

At three cents a share, it cost me $90, still percentagewise the best investment I ever made. It surprised even my experienced co-workers that options expired 60 days after you left a company, teaching me to read contracts very carefully.

I went to graduate school at the University of Washington, with a goal of working for Professor Craig Chambers. Craig Chambers and Urs Hoelzle were two Stanford PhDs who'd worked for David Ungar on the Self Programming language.

Urs went on to be Google's first Engineering Fellow. One of Craig's graduating students that year was Jeff Dean, who also became a Google Fellow. In fact, I'd often encounter my fellow graduate students again later in my career: Professor Chambers himself was eventually hired by Google.

Where are they now?

Reed Hastings became the co-founder and CEO of Netflix, and Neil Hunt is now Netflix's CPO. Reed also became a member of Microsoft's board of directors in 2007. Peng-Toh was a Senior Staff Engineer at Google by the time he retired. Steven Yen co-founded Kiva Software, which became Netscape Application Server after an acquisition.

Jeff Rothschild is currently VP of Technology at Facebook. Steven Grimm and Marc Kwiatkowski have retired from Facebook, while Larry Hastings is still at Facebook.

I consider myself very fortunate to have spent my career with so many luminaries, but my career isn't atypical. Silicon Valley is a very small place and, as previously mentioned, care should be taken not to burn any bridges with the smart people you meet during your career.

Unfortunately, Seattle weather didn't agree with me. I ended up falling ill three times a year, or once an academic quarter. When I fell ill during my third quarter finals, it was the last straw.

After I got well, I rode my bicycle to California for a summer job at Pure Software and never looked back. Later on, my doctor told me that, given my office job, I was Vitamin D deficient even under the California sun, possibly explaining why I got sick so often in Seattle.

Good weather is worth paying for.

During Pure Software's second year, it'd grown to about 90 employees. At that time, Microsoft was king of the hill, and I was put on a Windows product team trying to make it easier to deploy and instrument beta-programs for shrink-wrapped software. The product's natural audience was the large Windows software companies.

We hired engineers with Windows experience. As they were brought on board, the culture clash between them and the UNIX engineers left a deep impression on me.

The Windows engineers were self-taught programmers who didn't have time for computer science. PCs at the time were so slow with so little memory that deep knowledge of the platform was more important.

The UNIX programmers were used to powerful workstations with virtual memory, and most had a computer science degree (or three). The Windows engineers' lack of attention to computer science struck the UNIX folk as cavalier.

I enjoyed learning about new operating systems and got a chance to know both types of engineers quite well. As typical at startups, I moved from one desk to another quite often. One day fellow engineer Michael Curry, took me aside. I'd left my paystub in a desk he now used. He told me "They're not paying you enough, kid." I raised my eyebrow at that, and filed it away for reference.

Exchanging salary data with friends is a great way to know when you're underpaid and should start looking for another job

Ironically, Pure's IPO party was an extremely unhappy occasion for engineers. At the party, the CEO and VP of Engineering thanked all the financial-related employees and the sales employees, but didn't call out engineering for any attention. This sent a message that engineering wasn't appreciated, and the very next day you could almost hear the sounds of resumes being polished.

When an Mpath Interactive recruiter called me, I decided I'd at the very least interview there and find out what this fly-by-night internet startup was going to do.

After Pure Software made a bad acquisition of ClearCase, it was eventually bought by Rational Software, illustrating David Packard's saying that "more companies die of indigestion than starvation."

Mpath Interactive

In 1995, Jeff Rothschild and Brian Apgar were entrepreneurs-in-residence at different venture capital firms. An entrepreneur-in-residence (EIR) serves two functions. Usually, he's a technical resource for the VC partners, who have him perform due diligence on a startup or a proposed acquisition by one of the firm's funded companies. In addition, if the EIR develops a good idea for a startup, the firm would back him, getting in on a startup's ground floor with a founder that has a successful track record.

My Startup Story

Mpath Interactive started off as Brian Apgar's idea; he wanted to build a massively multiplayer online game. Jeff's idea was to put together an online business conferencing system. Since both online gaming and business conferencing require similar infrastructure, they exchanged business plans. While Jeff's plan would've been lower risk, both believed online gaming had the potential to be a much larger market. It was also more fun and exciting.

By the time I interviewed with Mpath, they'd hired two well-known game designers (Brian Moriarty and Danielle Bunton Berry) and several engineers (Marc Kwiatkowski, Steven Grimm, and Michael Wolf). Somehow, between when I interviewed and when I joined, the company morphed into a matchmaking service for gamers wanting low-latency connections to each other.

In 1995, DOS games were still common (few people remember the first versions of Warcraft and Quake only ran on a DOS box), and Mpath needed people who could make DOS games talk TCP/IP. The implementation tool for this was the VxD, or Virtual Device Driver.

Since VxDs ran in kernel mode, it could copy data between the DOS virtual machine address space and the Win32 user-mode programs. Thus, a system-call-like function call in a DOS program could trigger an RPC-like interface to talk to a user-mode Win32 program. This program then talked TCP over the wire to other machines, either in a peer-to-peer network or in client-server mode.

I interviewed with just one or two people at Mpath, and they made an offer. However, I didn't think much of the business of internet games. So I decided that it'd take a really good offer to get me to leave Pure, where I had three more years of vesting to go (though without very much stock).

At first, Mpath thought I was bluffing and decided they'd keep interviewing. However, the more they interviewed, the more they realized that VxD engineers were hard to come by, and therefore commanded high prices.

By the time I'd returned from a vacation, Mpath had worked themselves up to where they were willing to pay my asking price. I accepted the offer and gave notice at Pure.

Reed and my manager were shocked and immediately gave me a counter offer, but it fell short of Mpath's offer. I've since learned it's very common for new graduates to become underpaid within 2-3 years after graduation.

The only way to counteract this is to put together a peer group that compares salaries to better understand your relative position and where the market is. I did this with a couple of friends, and it served us well until we fell out of touch.

Having accepted Mpath's offer, I again had to go through the stock option exercise process. However, this came with a catch. Since Pure had just done an IPO, I couldn't sell any stock for six months.

For the first time in my life, I hired a tax accountant. He charged $250 an hour, and spent the hour explaining AMT, ISOs, how they interacted with each other, and the tax implications of exercising my stock options. In terms of bang for the buck, it was the best $250 I've ever spent. More important than his just doing my taxes, he gave me the intellectual tools required to understand how tax planning worked.

He also informed me that I didn't need to hire him as a tax preparer at $250/hour when a $40 copy of TurboTax would do just as good a job. "Just come back with your taxes when you're done, and we'll sit down over a sandwich and I'll go over it." He was true to his word.

Mpath was a blast. While Pure Software felt like a company filled with three-person projects that didn't often interact, Mpath felt like a large team with individuals working on smaller pieces.

The core team members, Steven Grimm, Michael Wolf, Dan Samuel, Marc Kwiatkowski, Jessica Koppel, and I worked so well together that at one point, we worked a full work week, spent a 3 day weekend on a sailing vacation where nearly everything went wrong, and were still happy to come back and work another four days together. When a team gets to work together for 2-3 years at a time, you get to know each other really well and develop a really high level of trust. Even if everything went wrong, no one blamed each other—all mistakes were approached dispassionately and everyone had a sense of being part of something bigger.

As someone who had to "port" games from other companies to Mpath's platform, I visited many game companies around the country, including some of the biggest names in the business; Id Software (yes, the DOS version of Quake had my code in it), Westwood Studios, Electronic Arts (in Canada, Washington, and other locations), and interacted with then-VP of Engineering at Blizzard Patrick Wyatt (a very nice guy who wrote great code).

My visits taught me something other game industry veterans already knew. The industry was flooded by enthusiastic and talented young engineers and thus didn't have to pay engineers by Silicon Valley standards. Since games were usually treated as one-off programs, coding standards were low (except at independent studios such as Id Software).

Those low standards resulted in many extremely badly written games. Hasbro's version of Scrabble, for instance, had network code that sent Windows messages over the wire (yes, the actual UI messages used to deal with menu items and key presses), rather than the game board, which would have been easier and much less bandwidth intensive. The typical B student at a major university wouldn't have made that mistake.

I needed more people as Mpath wanted to get more games on the platform, so I started an internship program. It turned out to be very successful, and Mpath got several hires out of it. These included some engineers we wouldn't have hired if we hadn't worked with them as interns.

After three and a half years at Mpath, Steven Yen asked if I'd like to join him at a new startup. Since Steve was the second smartest guy I knew in school (after Peng-Toh), I accepted without even knowing what the company was going to be about.

Mpath still wasn't profitable, but the dot.com bubble was inflating and allowed it to go public soon after I left. For a very short time, this made me a millionaire on paper.

Mpath changed its name to HearMe, then crashed along with the rest of the market, illustrating the importance of selling high. Especially if you own stock in a company that hasn't made any profits. Gamespy eventually purchased HearMe for pennies on the dollar.

When I showed Jeff an early draft of this book, he replied:

What is interesting from this episode is that the competition among entrepreneurs/VCs to have the first-mover advantage in a new market often causes companies to invest too early. Mpath would have been better off if this had happened 3-4 years later as it could have benefited from the growing base of broadband to the home and wouldn't have needed to focus on performance optimizations and network infrastructure that became largely irrelevant over time. For example sweating 2 bytes in headers and the PSINet Quality of Service work! Another example of this was the tablet/pen computing investments. 10 years later we had the iPhone. The technology just wasn't ready for the investments at the time.

Escalate

Formed just as the dot.com bubble peaked, Escalate meant to "reinvent" e-commerce. Keng Lim wanted to see how quickly he could build a company, wanting to scale it to 100 people in a year and generate business. The vision was to build an e-commerce platform that we'd sell as a service to other companies. The only problem was that Paul Graham had already built Yahoo! Stores, but Keng was convinced that larger companies with their own brand, such as Williams-Sonoma, would find Yahoo! Stores unsuitable.

Escalate's employment contract prohibited ownership in competing companies. I pointed out to Keng my 500 shares of Microsoft stock made this untenable, He agreed, changing the contract then and there.

Escalate was an exercise in building stuff quickly with known technologies, rather than inventing new tech, as Pure did. As its first employee, I had the privilege of helping select what technologies to rely on. We decided on Perforce as the source control system, Java as the primary language, and then proceeded to design the system.

As we recruited more engineers, we'd give them a piece of the system with an already specified interface and they'd build it. We ended up with a fully operational e-commerce system in six months, and were rolling out to customers within nine months.

In another illustration of what a small world this was, we interviewed and made an offer to Eric Veach, but he turned us down to join Google. Eric would go on to build and design several key Google ads systems, as well as the routing algorithm for Google Maps.

Silicon Valley is a small place. You'll likely encounter the same folks over and over again.

I helped recruit, interview and hire the engineers at Escalate. They were so high quality that when Escalate fell apart, most ended up at Yahoo and Google.

My biggest issue with Escalate was the commute. I lived in Saratoga and Escalate was in Redwood Shores. I had to buy a car (paid for by Mpath's IPO) for the commute, but it was nevertheless frustrating.

The drive took at least two hours a day, three hours when traffic was bad. After having a bike commute that made exercise part of my daily routine, a car commute was incredibly frustrating. Not only couldn't I work as hard as I used to, a bad commute made every day a different kind of hell. After just over two years, the frustration built up to the point where I had to quit my job just to regain some sanity.

Never deal with a bad commute if you can help it. Many studies have shown that a bad commute is even harder to adapt to than losing a limb.

Due to a shortage of paying customers, a few years after I left Escalate couldn't sustain further development. A customer eventually bought them.

Mirapoint

I quit my job in 2001, and traveled a bit before returning to Silicon Valley. I then interviewed with several different companies, with the most interesting position being managing Mirapoint's Applications group. At previous companies, I'd always been promoted to a first line manager. But this was an opportunity to be a manager from the beginning.

Unfortunately, after only three months, I was hit by a car on my bicycle commute home. This put me out of commission for several months, and I returned to work just before 9/11.

Mirapoint built mail appliances—servers you could just plug into your network, configure with a web browser, and then serve and route a company's e-mail. The industry thought it had the best back-end in the business. The system was built on top of FreeBSD.

The unfortunate problem and main barrier to sales was that most enterprises were hooked on Microsoft Exchange. The company ended up selling its product to Internet Service Providers (ISPs) that needed Mirapoint's high capacity servers.

The problem with this was that ISPs are in a low margin business, meaning customers would buy the minimum number of units and run them at maximum load. This resulted in a lot of customer support calls. One ISP even refused to pay until we threatened to visit their site and repossess all their machines.

At Mirapoint, I learned first hand that it sucked to be in the front-end team when the rest of the company was focused on the back-end. The team would get spurious bugs reported against the UI which boiled down to differences in taste (and the applications team would have all the UI, while the other teams would have text configuration files). Unfortunately, while the group was responsible for the UI, it never had the autonomy to make decisions for the UI, and the back-and-forth with the QA organization got to be very annoying.

Again and again, I longed for the days when I worked with Shelton Mar at Escalate. He always understood the business needs and would figure out a way to support the development and testing necessary, rather than sticking rigidly to testability. I would later hire Shelton Mar into Google, where he is currently a director of engineering.

One thing I learned at Mirapoint was how to negotiate. Since all the localization was done by external companies, we'd go back-and-forth on the price and get multiple vendors to bid against each other until either we got the lowest price possible or my time became more valuable than another few hundred dollars.

At one point, our localization vendor went bankrupt and asked us to pay for the last piece of work they did for us. My manager laughed and said, "They just took away any motivation that we might have had to pay them!"

Mirapoint couldn't sustain profitability and, despite a final funding round, was eventually liquidated.

Google

My old friend/roommate Peng-Toh and I ran into each other and he told me he was at Google. Intrigued, I paid him a visit. To my surprise, the smartest person I knew from school wasn't working on amazing search algorithms, but on machine monitoring software.

This wasn't a small job, since Google had entire buildings full of hardware. But while monitoring is important, it didn't require someone with Peng-Toh's talent implementing it. I thought that if Peng-Toh was stuck doing machine monitoring, I'd be sweeping the floor at Google.

After a bit of persuasion by Peng-Toh, I interviewed at Google for a release management position. Apparently, even after five years, Google didn't have a single release engineer.

During my interviews, I learned that Google really didn't know how to interview release managers, or really for any kind of management position. So interviewers asked me about search implementation instead.

The questions you can ask a manager about search are really limited, and the answers can be researched with just a few minutes of reading. But what's obvious to an engineer who's been immersed in search for years isn't obvious to anyone else, so I flunked out of the interview. Since Mirapoint was doing well at that time (having had a profitable year), I thought nothing of it and went on with my life.

Moving to Silicon Valley

Peng-Toh returned to Singapore after a year at Pure Software because he was bonded by the government which had paid for his Berkeley degree. After he fulfilled his contract there, he paid for his own plane ticket to Silicon Valley, stayed for 2 weeks, interviewed with 5 companies, and ended up with 5 job offers.

Sure, you're probably not as smart as Peng-Toh (I don't know very many people who are). But he had to fly from Singapore! If he can pull this off from across the Pacific Ocean, what excuse do you have for not doing it?

While recovering from my car-bike collision, I couldn't ride my bike and it was making me nuts. I thus stumbled back into a hobby I'd abandoned when I went to college; Dungeons and Dragons. After a while, I ended up playing D&D with a bunch of Googlers.

When Mirapoint fell on bad times and laid me off, Rob Shillingsburg and John Gregory from the D&D group talked me into giving Google Engineering another try. At the same time, I interviewed at Verisign and Yahoo!. Those both came to me through my Escalate contacts.

Surprisingly, Yahoo! had the toughest technical interview, and not surprisingly, Verisign had the easiest, despite that one being at an architect level. The reason the second Google interviews went better and so easily was probably because I was good at showing I could write code well, so my interviewers were impressed.

However, given what I know now about Google's interview process, it's conceivable that I had a stacked interview panel. For example, my first interviewer was Corey Anderson, one of my students when I was a teaching assistant at the University of Washington!

When the offers came in, I called up Jeff Rothschild and asked what he thought. He went through his analysis (basically, he assumed Google as a public company would be worth as much as Yahoo! and valued the stock options that way) and it was a no-brainer for me to join Google. He said "Furthermore, no matter what the stock option price is right now, I guarantee that it will be higher at the IPO."

I joined Google as an engineer. But on my first day, my manager, Bill Coughran said to me "As you might have guessed from reading the press, Google is preparing for an IPO. One of the gating factors is that we're missing a release engineering team, and with your experience, we would like you to do us the favor of helping us with that problem."

In the intervening year, Google still hadn't figured out how to interview release engineers, so Bill hacked around the culture by hiring an appropriately experienced engineer, and then putting him to work on the task.

Google's hiring process wasn't like any other company's that I'd interviewed at. Usually, most companies have a hiring manager set up interviews and also personally interview a candidate. Then that manager makes the final hire/no hire decision. Google reasoned that this led to undue pressure to just hire anybody, especially when there was too much work for too few engineers.

Urs Hoelzle proposed a system based on academia's hiring process. An interview panel was set up consisting almost entirely of engineers. Interviewers would provide independent written feedback on each candidate, which was entered into a database.

A separate hiring committee, also consisting of engineers, reviewed the feedback and made a hire/no-hire decision. Finally, for a larger number of years than you'd think, the founders personally made the final decision on every hire. They'd sometimes decide that no one but a software engineer was worth hiring. Only after all that would management get to decide

Promotions at Google

Promotions were also theoretically taken out of management's hands. Feedback was solicited from engineers' peers, then a panel of two levels higher engineers made the promotion decision. In practice, managers' feedback counted a lot, and a manager could torpedo your promotion chances by giving negative feedback.

This worked very well until more political minded engineers showed up and learned how to game the system (basically, you could form a clique and attack the system that way).

When I discussed this with Abhay Puri, a former Google Staff Engineer, he thought the biggest mistake was setting up an engineering ladder at all! As someone at a relatively high level on the ladder, he saw the different attitudes people had towards his ideas before and after he became a Staff Engineer and thought it was an unquestionably bad thing.

Fundamentally, creative activities like engineering are better driven through intrinsic motivation (having people do the best job they can because they're proud of it) rather than extrinsic motivation (having people work hard because they want the next promotion or bonus). After the engineering ladder was introduced, it took a while before extrinsic motivation started substituting for intrinsic motivation.

But once it happened, someone's eventually hired who was motivated to game the system. At that point, it's all over; the organization will be filled at the top levels with good politicians instead of good engineers.

It might be possible to design a promotion and reward system robust enough to survive smart people trying to game it. But so far, I've not heard of any company that's managed to do it.

compensation and make an offer.

This made the system more resistant to managers just hiring anyone they liked. Nevertheless, you could still game the system, if only by stacking the interview panel with people you knew were a good match for the candidate, either by field of interest or by personality.

When I started at Google, I immediately called up the release manager I'd worked with at Escalate and asked if he wanted to work with me to establish Google Release Engineering. He immediately sent me his resume. I forwarded it to Bill and Wayne Rosing (the VP of Engineering at the time) and said, "Let's get this guy."

Wayne was an expert at hacking the system. He set up an interview panel right away, and made sure he was an interviewer. He got all the feedback in right away, immediately put the package before the very next hiring committee meeting, and made the offer by the end of the week. The reason for the rush? He wanted the process over and done with before the founders got back from Europe.

To Wayne's credit, I never saw the process hacked except in this one case, and it wasn't egregious. If hires weren't getting arbitrarily dropped at the last minute, he wouldn't have had to do so at all.

It was an uphill struggle to hire release engineers until we got enough that Google understood what they were for, why they were needed, and what unique skills they brought to the engineering process.

In particular, I wanted to tread carefully. Engineering had gotten used to engineers being able to push a new release at any time, and the development process worked on that assumption. Release engineers wanted to control and constrain releases to reduce the risk of each new one. But they'd face opposition from teams adopting this new process if it was thought it slowed down the development and deployment cycle.

I took the approach of building release engineering as a service organization. Each new release engineer sat with an engineer during a release, documented each step, and learned how things were done. He'd then publish the document to the group, and then swap places with the engineer for the next release.

After three months, release engineers were in great demand. Now our problem was finding and hiring candidates flexible enough to cope with each team's completely different processes and idiosyncrasies.

In effect, unlike other companies where release engineers enforce policy, Google release engineers had to adapt processes to the already in place policies. These had organically grown in ad hoc manner over six years of operations. It took engineers capable of unusually flexible thinking to meet this challenge.

I did notice one thing. The purpose of the Sarbanes-Oxley regulation was to make it so that you'd need a conspiracy among multiple parties to embezzle money from a corporation. However, release engineering would get a handoff from development, perform the release step, deploy the code, and immediately hand back the production code to engineers. Adding only release engineers to the mix didn't make it any harder to embezzle.

Upon investigation, I discovered that Google did have engineers called Site Reliability Engineers (SREs) whose job it was to handle production. But the Ads group didn't have any! Ads generated the vast majority of Google's revenue (and still does), so I didn't think this situation was tenable. However, every time we hired a new SRE, they'd be allocated to Search.

I went to Wayne again, and said "Ads needs a separate pool of SREs." Wayne thought for a few seconds, then worked out my chain of reasoning aloud: "Every time we hire a new SRE, search grabs them. That's because search is also big and growing, and the chances of that diminishing over time are low. OK, we need a separate hiring pool for Ads SREs. Approved."

My jaw dropped. I expected to have to spend at least 10 minutes explaining my reasoning and arguing with Wayne about it—I'd never met a manager before who could reason so quickly through such structural decisions. That, combined with knowing how much revenue Google was generating, convinced me to exercise all my stock options the day after I got them. Even though doing so wiped out 3 years of cash savings.

However, after getting the approval I had to figure out what to do! Small companies lack resources to just open up a new hiring channel, but it's easy to get approval for necessary things. Large companies make it tough to get approval for doing new things, but once approved they usually have the bureaucracy and machinery to make them happen. Google was unique in having enough resources to approve things quickly, but didn't actually have the machinery or staffing to help a new employee execute their ideas.

It took me a few months to work myself into the SRE hiring process, getting an SRE requisition written, and hack the process for Ads SREs the way it was hacked for release engineers.

By the way, I didn't learn from experience. Later that year, I suggested on an internal mailing list that Google should have an internship program. I immediately got e-mail from Alan Eustace that it was a great idea and I should just set it up.

At a startup, be prepared to have to run with the ball on new ideas and projects

Management at Google was completely different from what I'd experienced. At one point, Bill decided the release engineering team should work with the Ads front-end group. Rather than explicitly tell us what to do, after we moved buildings Bill had us seated next to the Ads front-end group. We took the hint, and I especially appreciated his light managerial touch.

Google had hired such high quality people that these subtle hints could direct engineers, instead of needing the explicit command and control systems that lesser companies put into place. It wasn't unusual to go an entire quarter without meeting with your manager, but if you did, he'd know exactly what your project's status was.

After six months, I had a team of six release engineers in place, Google had publicly filed its earnings for the first time, and announced it would go public. My reward was getting to do software development again and join the search infrastructure team. I didn't know it then, but I'd stay at Google for more than six years, far longer than at previous employers.

Google's IPO was by far the most satisfying IPO I had experienced. While other companies had a big IPO party, Google treated it as just another working day. There was no celebration and no event to mark the occasion. While other companies had executives who showed up the day after an IPO with brand new Porsches, Wayne threatened to take a baseball bat to the car of any engineer who drove in with an ostentatious model.

Other companies underwrote their IPOs with traditional investment banks that severely underpriced their stock (by as much as 75% in the case of Netscape). This effectively took money from shareholders and gave it to investment bankers. Google used an auction IPO method instead that fairly priced its stock.

My previous IPOs had locked up all employees' stock for six months after the IPO. Google managed to negotiate with the SEC and investment banks to allow employees to sell 5% of their holdings after a month, and another 10% after three months.

Ironically, unlike my previous IPOs, those who held on after the first six months received ample capital gains. But given how many had been at Google for six years and had thousands or hundreds of thousands of shares via two stock splits, it was understandable that asset diversification outweighed any other consideration.

However, there was a complication. The SEC investigated Google for underpricing its stock options in its final year as a private company. Google negotiated a settlement, where employees who hadn't exercised their stock options had to file a 409A election. This generally meant that they had to decide before the start of the year how much stock they had to exercise and then dispose of the stock, not always with their preferred timing. Those of us who exercised all our stock options were exempted from this ruling.

If you work at a hot pre-IPO company that's very profitable, immediately exercise all your options.

Further reading

Startup: A Silicon Valley Adventure. Jerry Kaplan, Penguin 1996. A story of a failed startup, told from the founder's point of view. (http://goo.gl/9CUb)

Almost Perfect. W. E. Pete Peterson, http://www.wordplace.com/ap/ One of WordPerfect's early employees tells the story of a company that succeeded beyond any of its founders' dreams, but in the end didn't build a management structure capable of handling the scale it needed to operate at. (http://goo.gl/Yqom)

Stumbling on Happiness. Daniel Gilbert, Vintage 2007. A scientific explanation of why we're unhappy. It explains why people with a bad commute are less happy than even people who've lost limbs. (http://goo.gl/xXJL)

High-tech Ventures: The Guide For Entrepreneurial Success. C. Gordon Bell, John E. Mcnamara, Basic Books, 1991. (http://goo.gl/TJyQ)

Acknowledgements

Writing is said to be a lonely task, but it's much less lonely with an internet connection and enthusiastic friends who double as proof-readers to help out.

I'm in debt to the following for their help in improving the book's ideas and text (alphabetically by last name): Jim Ausman, Kevin Chang, Stephen Chen, Marya Doery, Tom Galloway, Arthur Gleckler, Larry Hosken, Case Larsen, XiaoQin Ma, Ovidiu Predescu, Kekoa Proudfoot, Jeff Rothschild, Fritz Schneider, Arun Sharma, Peng-Toh Sim, Santhosh Srinivasan, Cynthia Wong, Hector Yee and Cindy Zhou. XiaoQin gave me the idea to expand on the green card section, and Cindy and Santhosh provided additional help.

Larry Hosken took on the incredibly painful job of copyediting all the editions of this book. Tom Galloway did a sentence by sentence edit of the second edition (including this acknowledgment!), and provided extensive corrections as well as tightening my prose. Any sentences that flow particularly well are Tom and Larry's. All the awkward sentences are mine.

Kevin Chang did extensive work on the book's website, for which I will be eternally grateful. Lisa Wong provided extensive help with the book's formatting. Special thanks also to Brian Apgar, Arthur Gleckler, Larry Hosken, Jeff Rothschild, Abhay Puri, Wayne Rosing, Fritz Schneider and Peng-Toh Sim for allowing me to quote them.

Scarlet Tang re-designed the cover for the 3rd Edition.

Index

Made in the USA
Middletown, DE
11 October 2020